Winging It

A Story of Love, Loss, and Fifty Chickens

Pauline Buck

Winging It

Some of the names have been changed to protect the "guilty." The author's law student friend suggested all the names be changed, but the author, having lived with a professional actor for over thirty years, knew that for some people, credits are a must.

A portion of proceeds from the sale of this book will be donated to the Alzheimer Society of B.C. to be allocated to the support programs they offer families and people living with Alzheimer's.

All photos from the author's personal archives unless otherwise credited
Author photo: I. Bird
Editing: Naomi Pauls, Paper Trail Publishing

The prologue was read in an earlier form on CBC Radio's *Sunday Edition*, September 24, 2017. The quote that appears at the start of Part II is excerpted from Jane Fonda's 2011 TED talk, *Life's Third Act,* https://www.ted.com/talks/jane_fonda_life_s_third_act?language-en.

Tellwell Talent
www.tellwell.ca

ISBN
978-0-2288-6699-2 (Paperback)
978-0-2288-6700-5 (eBook)

For Bill

CONTENTS

AUTHOR'S NOTE

WINGING IT HAS BEEN A five-year labour of love that had its origins over ten years ago. In 2008, I moved with my husband Bill from a Vancouver high-rise to a five-acre hobby farm in the heart of the Fraser Valley, British Columbia's prime agricultural region. To keep our friends in the loop and save myself from the need to write copious emails about our radical lifestyle change, I started a private blog called *Home on the Ranch*, in which I regaled everyone with tales of our rural adventures. Over time, the blog posts changed to include more information about Bill's worsening dementia and my feelings during this difficult time. The record I kept of those years was helpful when I was putting together this memoir.

* * *

They say it takes a village to raise a child. Similarly, I've learned over the past five years that it takes a team to produce a book. And I have been fortunate to have had an excellent and caring team behind me through this memoir-writing journey. Its first members were the regular readers of the blog posts that I bashed out to friends who were curious to know how two city slickers could possibly survive life on a farm. Many of those readers encouraged me to compile into a book my amusing stories of our farmer wannabe capers and poignant posts about Bill's dementia and life after his loss. Thank you, all, for starting me down this road.

Next came award-winning editor Barbara Pulling, who reviewed my first draft and sent back positive comments and notes that answered my initial question to her, "Is there something worth publishing here or should I just throw it in the bottom drawer and let my daughter find it after I'm dead?"

Five years and I've lost count of how many drafts later, this finished version is thanks to the suggestions and tips from friends and family beta readers; plus the caring feedback and insightful comments from members of the writers' group I'm grateful to belong to: Libby Davies, Luiza Shankulova, Margaret Stott and Alexandra Wilson. We five met at a memoir writing class at the University of British Columbia and get together regularly to encourage each other's work.

Thanks to Daphne Gray-Grant's Get It Done! program, I stayed the course when the thought of producing yet another set of rewrites became overwhelming. Daphne also looked over the "latest" draft and recommended I engage editor Naomi Pauls to take *Winging It* to the finish line. Naomi not only caught the typos and spelling errors and sorted out the chronological mix-ups (her math is much better than mine), she also helped me see where some of my thoughts were a bit convoluted and suggested some word revisions for clarity. Yay, Naomi.

And, of course, thanks to my family, who whole-heartedly encouraged us to move out to the farm, offered great help with the ins and outs of rural living, and provided me with the support I needed during Bill's illness.

Last but not least, thanks to Michael Cowhig, a friend and enthusiastic and exceedingly talented photographer who understands the intricacies of image technology and happily offered to format the pictures I had chosen to include in the book.

My heartfelt appreciation to everyone who assisted me on this journey to publication, including some I've probably forgotten to name. I doubt I'd have made it to print without your unflagging encouragement. Thank you, all, and enjoy the read.

PROLOGUE

It finally happened. I knew it would. I just didn't know when. Bill and I were driving back to our farm after being out for an hour or so, picking up groceries and running errands.

"That's our house there, on the right," said my husband as we got close to home. Rather dryly, I responded, "Yes, I know. We've lived here for three years."

"We have?" he asked.

I turned to look at him directly, to see if he was kidding me, and saw that he was not. His face, straight and serious, looked a bit puzzled.

"Do you know who *I* am?" I asked, hoping against hope that my worst fear so far had not materialized.

"No," he said. "Who are you?"

It's hard to describe how I felt at that moment. Panic-stricken, I guess. Not to mention heartbroken. Friends had been asking whether Bill still recognized me, and I had been shrugging off their question with a quick "Of course." I wondered if I'd been in denial about his condition for the past three years. Did I think he really didn't have dementia? That he was just having a few bad days?

By now the signs of his illness were obvious. Bill attended adult daycare Wednesdays and Fridays so I could go in to the office; we had visits from a home care worker twice a week, plus support from a case manager at the regional health authority. After regular visits to the doctor for memory tests, Bill's dosage of dementia medication had been increased every few months.

Just bad days? A lot of bad days. But they had provided a great excuse for me to work from home part time, avoiding a daily commute to the city and giving me a chance to spend more time with Bill. I had convinced myself his confusion would all go away as soon as I retired at the end of the year, and we would have lots of fun again then. In hindsight, yes, I was in serious denial.

Still in shock as I pulled into the driveway on this October afternoon in 2011, I decided to resort to one of my two main coping mechanisms:

humour (i.e., laughing it off) and faking it (pretending everything was normal). I chose faking it. We entered the house and together unloaded the groceries as if nothing was wrong. Because it was a wet and chilly day, I turned on the gas fireplace, and we sat down at the coffee table in the living room to work on our jigsaw puzzle.

After a few minutes of silence, Bill said, "You're a very nice person." I nodded a sort of thank-you. Then he picked up the TV remote control and tried to dial out with it. He often got the remote mixed up with the portable telephone, which could make things tricky when he was trying to answer a call.

"Who are you phoning?"

"Pauline," said Bill. "It's not like her to not call on her way home."

Now I was really in a panic. I finally said, "*I* am Pauline, your wife. We've been married for twenty-two years."

The look Bill gave me was incredulous. "You are? We have? Why didn't I know?" So I went back to being quiet and found a few more jigsaw pieces that fit. Hell, I needed something to fit!

Later, after dinner, Bill returned to his theme. He said he really loved his wife and if it weren't for her, he would be quite interested in me because I was so nice. But he wanted me to know that we could never have anything together because he was happily married. I must say, that comment made my day. But, as I realized bedtime was approaching, a wave of fear washed over me. If Bill did not think I was his wife, then where were we going to sleep? *Would he try to push me out of bed?*

In the bathroom, I got out the vitamins I take at night. "Pauline has a little holder just like that for her vitamins too," said Bill. My desperate response was an interested-sounding "Oh, yes." I did not want to say anything that might upset Bill. I wasn't physically afraid—I outweighed him and I was stronger—but I had heard that some people with dementia could get aggressive or even violent if others argue with them too much or keep telling them they are wrong. So, keeping conversation to a minimum, I kept my nightly routine as normal as possible. After putting on my pyjamas, I threw my clothes into the laundry basket in the closet, as I always did.

"Pauline does all our laundry," said Bill. "She'll wonder about those clothes in there."

"Oh, I'm sure she'll be fine with it," I said cautiously.

The actual showdown came when I got into the bed. Bill stood in the middle of the room and asked what I was doing. I said I was going to sleep, to which he replied, "But you can't sleep there. That's my wife's place." At this point I took a big gamble and said, speaking slowly, "I know you don't understand this, because you have a disease in your brain and you can't help it, but *I am your wife.* I am Pauline. If you don't want to sleep with me, you can go sleep in the spare room. I don't plan to give up my bed."

"Oh," said Bill, and came to bed quietly. *Phew!*

The next day the question of who I was never came up. Around noon my daughter, Dianne, and her husband, Mike, our family supporters, popped in for coffee. While they were visiting, Bill was noticeably quiet—I don't think he said a word—but at least he didn't ask them who they were. And when they were gone, he commented on something Dianne had said, mentioning her by name. That was a relief. As for me? I didn't know who I was to Bill that day. Back in "faking it" mode, I was afraid to ask.

PART I

The best laid schemes o' mice an' men
Gang aft a-gley.

—Robert Burns, "To a Mouse"

CHAPTER 1

In the beginning

BILL BUCK WAS MY SECOND husband. We met in January 1984. When people used to ask me how we got together, I loved to say I hired him and then kept him. Then, if they knew he was a professional actor, I would add, "Fortunately, after a year he stopped charging me residuals."

I was working as an account executive at Miller Wilson, a Vancouver-based PR firm. Our team had hired a comedy writer to create a skit for one of our clients to present at their annual customer appreciation breakfasts, which were held in Vancouver and Victoria. I was in charge of production, which meant I looked after just about everything that nobody else wanted to do. The five-member cast for the skit comprised mostly people from our office and the client's office. But for insurance I had also hired one professional comic, Bill Reiter, to boost the quality of the overall performance in case the rest of us froze onstage. About a week before our first "opening night"—or opening morning, in this case—somebody backed out of the cast, and no amount of cajoling or arm-twisting on my part could convince any of the other staff members to join our thespian group. We were short one of the skit's crucial roles.

Bill Reiter suggested I call his friend Bill Buck, a professional actor he had worked with. The two Bills had performed in *Dr. Bundolo's Pandemonium Medicine Show* on CBC, a crazy weekly Monty Python–style variety show of political satire and just plain nonsense that ran from 1972 to 1979 on radio, two more seasons on television, and then was reprised in the Canada Pavilion for six weeks during Expo 86, Vancouver's world's fair. In *Bundolo*, Bill (Buck) performed as the "straight man" to the three incorrigible comedians in the cast, Bill Reiter, Norm Grohmann, and Marla Gropper. He was described in a *Vancouver Broadcasters* article that featured the history of the *Bundolo* show as a "comic anomaly" whose "conservative, nattily groomed ... Dudley Dooright, cleancut Canadian square niceness ... prove[d] vital to the chemistry" of the *Bundolo* group.

Bill (Buck) also acted regularly in many of the weekly hour-long American television series that were being shot in Vancouver, and he occasionally landed a part in one of the locally produced American feature films that were benefiting from Vancouver's excellent production capabilities. In addition, Bill appeared live onstage in local Arts Club Theatre productions.

Crossing my fingers, I called him about the skit. "You don't know me but...," I began and then explained the bind I was in. To my relief, Bill said he might be available to join us and asked when I would need him to show up for a meeting and possible start to rehearsals. "Our next rehearsal is this afternoon at four," I told him. His immediate response was, "You are desperate, aren't you?"

"Yes."

"Okay, I'll come." I thanked him and, as I signed off, breathed a huge sigh of relief.

Just before four that afternoon, Bill arrived at our office. I was immediately impressed when I saw him standing in the reception area and felt our little production would be in good hands. He emitted an aura of casual confidence that fit perfectly with his jeans, warm-looking jacket, and well-worn sneakers. His slim frame, just shy of six feet, was genuinely nice-looking. Not drop-dead gorgeous—just nice. Oh, yes, I liked his smiling blue eyes and full head of curly brown hair too. And then there was his voice. When I heard his rich baritone say "Hi. I'm Bill Buck," I made a mental note to call him to voice any commercials we were producing.

Taking him into our board room's makeshift rehearsal space, I introduced Bill to the others in the cast, then handed him a script, saying, "You'll play the newspaper publisher." I was playing the part of the media mogul. "Fine," he said, and we started the rehearsal. Needless to say, I now had a full cast and everything went well. After our production, the client was really happy, which pleased me as well. The next week I wrote Bill a heartfelt thank-you letter and closed the file on this project. Next thing I knew, Bill called and invited me out for lunch. That was the real beginning of our thirty-year life together.

Our relationship started slowly, which I liked. I was a single mother in my thirties at the time. My thirteen-year-old daughter and I had been living on our own since she was eighteen months old, when my first husband hightailed it back to his Belfast home after our rather tumultuous four-year marriage broke up. Unlike other single mothers that I met along the way, I was not saddled with a difficult-to-get-along-with ex. Mine was six thousand miles away, and while he did not contribute anything financial to our life, he also did not create any problems. He was totally out of the picture.

Dianne and I shared our rented two-bedroom townhouse on Vancouver's North Shore with Sheena, a very spoiled Afghan hound. With a young teenager at home, I needed to be mindful of my dating activities. Since my divorce, my love life had been somewhat spotty. I had dated a bit but for the most part, the majority of my social life came from the volunteer activities I enjoyed. I was involved in an organization called Vancouver AM, comprising members of the hospitality industry who organized events and activities that vigorously promoted Vancouver as a tourist destination. I also sat on the board of the Lions Gate Medical Research Foundation.

For about three months after our first lunch, Bill and I only got together every couple of weeks, usually for dinner after work. I'd meet him somewhere downtown or at his condo on the west side of Vancouver, then take myself back home. We talked on the phone a lot though. He loved talking on the phone. At least twice a week he'd call and we'd yak for about an hour. Okay, I like talking on the phone too. He didn't seem to be in a rush to dive right into a serious relationship and neither was I, which gave us time to get to know each other.

By spring, my girlfriends were getting really curious about this Bill person I talked about. I myself was wondering whether this friendship would ever develop into anything more. I really liked Bill, and so did Dianne. I had invited him over to our place a couple of times for dinner, and he became an instant hit when he offered to walk Sheena for Dianne one rainy night. Finally, in June, I got my first clue that Bill had more-than-friendship feelings for me. He told me he had been invited to a friend's wedding and asked whether I would like to go with him. "Sure," I said. "When is it?" *Would I have time to find a new outfit?* "September," he said. *September,* I thought. *This is June. We're still going to be together in three months? How wonderful. We must be an item.*

When we were first seeing each other, I loved being part of a couple; being able to go places and do things with someone. And being part of a couple with Bill as the other half made me especially happy. I loved introducing him to my friends. They instantly warmed to his easygoing manner and sense of humour, which did my sense of self-esteem a lot of good and enhanced our social life greatly. He loved to laugh and enjoyed being in lively company. He was also a hit with my family. My mom and her husband, George, were delighted to meet my "new boyfriend," and we got together with them for dinner quite often. As we got to know each other, I soon realized that with Bill, what you saw was what you got. He didn't put on airs or pretend he was something he was not. (Unless it was in the script, of course.) In real life, he was down-to-earth—real. I also learned early in our friendship that he was very caring. Shortly after we met his mom passed away, and Bill was genuinely concerned for his eighty-two-year-old dad, who suddenly found himself living alone in the home he and his wife had shared for over forty years. Bill visited him a lot and was available any time his dad needed anything. Sometimes we both went over to see him or help with something.

When we started getting serious, Bill told me he had wanted a lasting relationship in the past but had not met the right person. He had been seriously involved twice over the years, but for one reason or another, neither relationship had worked out. I too had hoped to meet a permanent partner, one who was happy to share our lives together, and who wouldn't be perturbed by the fact that I had a child. Bill and I were a good fit. Over the period of eighteen months since our first meeting in my office, we had developed a loving relationship that admired and respected each other's talents and loved and enjoyed each other's persona. Professionally, I was able to cast Bill's voice and acting talent in a few radio commercials for clients at work. And he was a supportive sounding board for me at the end of a busy day.

On October 15, 1985, Bill moved in. Even though we both wanted to be together, we thought a trial run would be a good idea. Bill was fifteen years older than I was—54 to my 39—but his energy and looks denied it. Our age spread was never an issue. Before getting snagged by me and Dianne, he had never been married or even lived with a woman. Bill had no kids of his own. His passion was acting. After whetting his appetite in Vancouver's community theatre, he had left town while in his early twenties for England, to train at the London Academy of Music and Dramatic Arts. After completing the program, he worked in Great Britain as a professional actor for seven years. Cast as "the American" in British-made movies and television shows, he also appeared in live productions around the country. He had returned to Vancouver in 1967 to participate in some of the Canadian Centennial productions.

With me bringing a built-in family to the table, plus dog, our new living arrangement was a risky proposition for us both. Instead of selling it, Bill rented out his condo and we crowded all of his furniture into my place, in case he needed to move it all back. (Good thing my townhouse had a fair-size basement. A living room can only handle so many chesterfields and end tables.) Dianne thought Bill's arrival was excellent because he brought with him a VCR, something which, according to her, we needed badly. She also thought it was cool that she could turn on the TV and see Mom's boyfriend in locally produced shows such as *21 Jump Street*, *MacGyver*, or *Danger Bay*. Since most kids in her class came from blended families, for Dianne it was no big deal that Bill was now a live-in. She liked him and so did her friends.

Looking back on those early days, though, I can't help but think, *Poor Bill.* He didn't know what he was getting himself into. Life with a hormone-laden teenager and an exceedingly independent single mom who had been ruling the roost forever was new territory for him. When he moved in, I'm sure he was visualizing himself as Robert Young on the fifties sitcom *Father Knows Best.* Silly him. Or perhaps he'd watched too many *Leave It to Beaver* reruns and thought he would make a great Ward Cleaver. He might have, had the culture not moved on. Had children not become allowed to have opinions and express them vehemently at the dinner table. He often whispered to me, "She talks so much, and what she's saying isn't right." I had to explain that Dianne's opinions were based on a mere thirteen years of life, and it was logical they would be different from our own. I further said that she was used to being a major part of any conversation in the house.

I had not realized that I too would have to make some concessions to this new situation. All of a sudden, my word wasn't necessarily the "last say." I had to learn how to consult. Hmm. There was a concept. After we'd been living together a little over a year, Bill and I decided to get some advice from a counsellor. We loved one another, and we wanted our relationship to work, but we each had baggage that needed unpacking. We were both only children who were used to having our own way—and we each thought we were right—which was leading to conflict. Added to the mix was another only child, mine, whom it would seem I wasn't quite as willing to share as I thought I was. With the help of Beverley Pugh, an excellent clinical counsellor, we worked through our personal issues. Meanwhile, Dianne was basically oblivious to most of the angst, with her priorities revolving around what her friends were doing.

CHAPTER 2

Early signs

FOR THE NEXT TWENTY YEARS, Bill and I had a super life. We soon divested ourselves of all the duplicate furniture, and within a year we moved from my rented townhouse to one we purchased close by, staying within the school district for Dianne. We were able to climb aboard the real estate train that was taking off after Expo 86 because Bill came up with the down payment. Until then, purchasing a home had been beyond my means.

Like most people in the entertainment industry, Bill had a day job. He actually had two. At the Joseph L. Crane Memorial Library at the University of British Columbia, he read textbooks onto tape for students who were blind or visually impaired. The hours of that job were flexible enough that he could still be available for auditions or performances. His other source of income was the taxi business. Having started as a part-time driver when he moved back to Vancouver, he had progressed to being the owner of two Yellow Cabs, both car and licence, which were lucrative investments. When we decided to purchase a place of our own, he produced the down payment by selling one of the cabs and also his apartment.

Our new home was a twenty-five-year-old three-storey townhouse with three bedrooms, a balcony off the master bedroom, and a nicely landscaped deck and sitting area out back off the kitchen—perfect for barbecuing. We didn't have to do much except change the colours of the walls and replace the carpets. Bill's dad offered to give us new flooring throughout, a gift we were delighted to receive. By the time we had moved in, I knew that Bill and Dianne were good together, but I had no idea they would bond over a bottle of Worcestershire sauce. Once a month I attended an evening client meeting, leaving them to fend for themselves for dinner. Getting home around my usual 9:00 p.m. on one of those evenings, I noticed an aura of slightly tense excitement in the air. Bill and Dianne were both in the living room, ostensibly watching television, but their "Hi. How was your meeting?" sounded a tad forced. My spidey sense suddenly alerted, I said, "Fine," and warily headed into the kitchen to find the leftovers they had put away for me. Nothing seemed amiss. But something was.

When I took my plate into the dining room, Bill and Dianne were standing beside the table looking worriedly down at the rug. "Okay," I said. "What happened?" Turns out the lid on the bottle of Worcestershire sauce was not on tight, and during dinner one of them shook it. (I never found out which one.) The spray made a geometrically perfect dark brown arc across our brand new pearl-grey wall-to-wall broadloom. Dashing for the phone book, they called the carpet cleaner whose Yellow Pages ad shouted "Emergencies Welcome" and guaranteed results or your money back. Long story short, the technician came, applied his magic formula that did indeed remove the stain, and left, saying that if the mark came back when the spot was dry, he'd return to clean it again. By the time I got home, the rug had started to dry and was remaining spotless. I had no idea what *they* had to pay for this fabulous service, but as the evening wore on, they began to look more and more relieved. Next morning all was well, and Bill and Dianne were joined at the hip from then on.

In the early 1990s, after Dianne had finished her post-secondary education and moved into her own apartment, we sold the townhouse on the North Shore and moved into Vancouver. We bought a one-bedroom, 1,600-square-foot condo in a brand new high-rise on Quebec Street. The first of a group of condo towers on the former site of Expo 86, City Gate was located on the north side of False Creek, right across from Science World. Because the building was new and most of the suites were large, our address quickly became a sought-after location for interior shots in the many movies and television shows being produced in Vancouver. When our building's strata council was first approached by a film's location manager, knowing Bill was experienced with the film industry, it contacted him for some how-to advice. He readily became the liaison between the production companies and the building, helping a number of our neighbours negotiate contracts for the use of their apartments. Ours was used once too. I loved watching the crew set up—two hours for a five-minute scene!

The urban environment of our new home worked well for us. We were two SkyTrain stops from the hub of downtown Vancouver's entertainment and shopping areas, not to mention Bill's agent's office. Bill's commute to UBC was 20 minutes faster than before and didn't include any traffic-infested bridges, and my office was an easy 30-minute walk from home, a pleasant form of commute I often chose. Situated just minutes away from Chinatown and Gastown, two of the city's popular tourist attractions, our suite had an unobstructed view of False Creek, which was home each summer to the Vancouver Dragon Boat Festival and provided part of the route for the colourfully lit carol ships every Christmas. We were also just a block away from the Downtown Eastside, a neighbourhood fraught with many complex social issues, including poverty and homelessness. While we loved our apartment and being surrounded by the rapid development under way, we hoped, perhaps naively, that the gentrification taking place would not negatively impact the low-income long-term residents of the surrounding area.

A year or so after we moved into City Gate, Bill was thrilled to walk Dianne down the aisle. No father of the bride could have beamed brighter than he did as he escorted her up to her husband-to-be. And no parents could have been happier with their new son-in-law than we were. From the first time we met Mike, we liked him a lot and hoped he would be "the one."

As a couple, Bill and I socialized a lot with many friends: the great group of people in the entertainment business that Bill brought into our life, plus my friends and colleagues and folks we met along the way, all of whom blended well with each other. We loved hosting or attending parties and casual get-togethers and also going to shows—either the big Broadway touring musicals or locally produced plays. We also did a bit of travelling—to Hawaii, Mexico, Europe, the United States, and Britain. Our most exciting trip was in November 1987, a fourteen-day tour of what was then the Soviet Union with a group of sixteen Canadian actors, producers, directors, and writers. We were part of a Canadian/Russian exchange program of people in the entertainment world. During the tour our group visited famous cultural landmarks such as the Bolshoi Theatre in Moscow and the Kirov Ballet school in St. Petersburg. We also toured historic mosques in the southern provinces of Uzbekistan and Kazakhstan. It was in the city of Samarkand that Bill changed my life again.

Our bus had pulled up to Guri Amir, the beautifully restored Persian mausoleum of the exalted Mongol conqueror of the fourteenth century, Tamerlane the Great. Despite being late in the year, this day was warm and sunny. Rather than join the group inside another traditional but chilly place of worship, Bill and I had chosen to stay outside, enjoying the balmy November breeze. After a minute or two, I realized Bill had gone quiet. Noticing a rather strange look on his face, I said, "You look like you're about to say something significant." After a beat, he said, "Will you marry me?" *Yes* was my immediate response. I was really surprised and excited. I definitely preferred to be married in spite of the acceptance and popularity of common-law relationships, and Bill did too. We had talked about getting married, but I had no idea Bill had planned to propose on this trip. He said later that his original idea was to do the complete "down on the knee" bit in the middle of Red Square, in Moscow. However, when we were there, he'd been deterred by the freezing-cold weather and the seriously armed militia marching in the vicinity of Lenin's Tomb. That's how Uzbekistan got upgraded to the proposal location of choice. When we got back home, we had my engagement ring specially designed with three half-carat diamonds in a row, the centre stone being from Russia.

Gotta love wedding cake

On Saturday, March 15, 1989, we were married by Rev. Alan Reynolds, the United Church minister at University Hill Congregation, which worships in the Chapel of the Epiphany, on the edge of the UBC campus. Alan, formerly the senior minister at Vancouver's Ryerson United Church, had been my pastor since Dianne was a baby, although my attendance at Sunday services was a bit hit-and-miss because we didn't live close to Alan's church. But when we were there, I loved his sermons. It always felt like he was speaking directly to me. Over the years he faithfully kept in touch, checking in to see how we were doing and arranging the occasional lunch. He always said that when I got remarried, he wanted to perform the service—delightfully optimistic of him, I thought. So when I agreed to marry Bill, my acceptance came with a caveat. We couldn't get married unless Alan officiated, and he had since moved from Ryerson. A little sleuthing later, Bill discovered Alan's parish was just around the corner from Bill's job at Crane Library. It was an exciting reunion the Sunday morning when Bill and I appeared, unannounced, at University Hill to tell Alan about our engagement. We were married the following March.

Our wedding was a lovely affair, with a gathering of supportive and happy friends from our eclectic crowd and my family, Bill's dad being unable to attend. Standing up with me were my lifelong friend Elaine as matron of honour, and Dianne, who was a beautiful bridesmaid. Bill's best man was his long-time friend Bruce, who was honoured to return the favour, since Bill had sung at his wedding many years before. Elaine's husband John served as the official usher. The reception at the University Golf Course gave the *Bundolo* crowd more opportunities to one-up themselves during the speeches, but Bill won the day in the smart remarks department. The next day we flew to Hawaii for our honeymoon. For a wedding gift, Mom and George had upgraded our economy tickets to business class both ways, so we started married life up the circular stairway in the dome section of the plane, relaxing in the spacious seats while enjoying the gourmet meal and excellent wine provided.

Over time, Bill and I became active members of the Uhill congregation. (Alan had a knack for recruiting people to get involved.) Bill, having spent his formative years in Sunday school, like most of the kids of that era, was happy to join in. He regularly served as Sunday morning lector, his rich voice bringing the scriptures to life, and also delivered the homilies or messages written for musical services presented by River City Gospel Jazz, a group of musicians that Alan, an inveterate trombone player and jazz lover, had formed. I, meanwhile, found myself sitting on various congregational committees.

Before we were married, Dianne's friends used to call me "Mrs. A," my last name being Armstrong. But what to call Bill? "Mr. Buck" just wasn't him. And "Bill" was a tad too informal for the teenagers coming and going in the house. It was Dianne's friend Tammy who coined the name that stuck with Bill for the rest of his life. He became "Mr. Bill." Everyone, including some of his friends and even my mother, who was crazy about him, called him Mr. Bill. Dianne called him Dad.

Changing my last name from Armstrong to Buck was not an easy decision for me. By 1989, many if not most newly married women did not take on their husband's name. When I married the first time, I automatically switched from being Pauline King to Pauline Armstrong. Women's lib notwithstanding, I liked the name Armstrong. It went well with my first name and was easy to pronounce and spell. Occasionally, though, I got called Pauline Johnson instead. And probably not because the person addressing me was a lover of poetry or chocolate. Most likely it was because they remembered my last name was Anglo Saxon, two syllables, easy to say, and familiar—*Oh, it must be Pauline Johnson.*

By the time Bill and I were engaged, I was established professionally in various local communications sectors as "Pauline Armstrong," and that was the name of the Vancouver-based PR firm I had formed, Pauline Armstrong Communications Inc. There were advantages to becoming Pauline Buck even though I liked the name Armstrong, not the least of which was that I knew Bill (secretly) would like it, even though he never asked me to change my name. I was really happy to be getting married and wanted everyone to know about it. What better way than to arrive everywhere announcing a new name? And, if the president of Pauline Armstrong Communications had a different name from the name of the company, the company's image would seem larger—less like the two-person operation it was. Opportunistic? Sure. Why not? Buck was a good name—easy to pronounce, Anglo Saxon, and only one syllable. So after some deliberation and a few practice goes at a new signature, I happily became Mrs. B.

As our relationship grew and flourished, so did my career. In the late 1980s, I left Miller Wilson, and for the next six years I ran my own communications business. With a rented office in the premises of a friend and the help of one assistant, I attracted a number of interesting clients. First through my door was Perimeter Transportation, the bus company that ferried passengers back and forth between downtown Vancouver hotels and the airport. The company wanted to announce the renewal of its provincial contract. Since this was back in the dark ages—with no internet, social media, or even fax machines—I got the message out the old-fashioned way. I arranged a 7:00 a.m. media conference on board one of Perimeter's buses. The event involved decorating the bus with balloons and organizing a breakfast box for reporters from one of the hotels. While the company president made his announcement through the on-board sound system, the bus driver circled the city, stopping briefly at each hotel the company served. Bill offered to help me attach the balloons, but as he was climbing up the ladder to the top of the bus, balloons in hand, he suddenly said, "Why am I doing this? This bus is my competition. I own a taxi." Upshot? The contract renewal story got front-page coverage in the morning paper, and Bill proved, yet again, what a great guy he was.

Other contracts of my own included publicizing productions of Theatre Under the Stars—great fun to work on every summer. For the Ministry of Transportation and Highways, I provided media training seminars for personnel around the province. With the 1990s advent of laptops, cellphones, and email, I moved my business home and went freelance. Much of my work then focused on health care communications, and I did projects for the major hospitals in Vancouver. With retirement starting to loom around the corner, and thoughts of a guaranteed pension plan popping into my head, in 2004 I accepted a full-time job as communications manager for the BC Branch of the Kidney Foundation of Canada, a position I held until my sixty-fifth birthday.

* * *

It was around 2002 that Bill's behaviour started to change. He became lethargic and disinterested in most of what was going on around him. He also started getting confused. We had arranged a month-long house exchange with friends who lived forty kilometres east of Bordeaux in a restored farmhouse situated on half an acre near the town of Bergerac, in the Dordogne region of France. After purchasing their retirement dream, our friends had worked diligently to upgrade and renovate the interior while maintaining the integrity of its era. The result was a traditional eighteenth-century heritage home with period furnishings, modern appliances, and tasteful decor. When we were there, Bill wasn't interested in participating in any sightseeing or local village activities, and sometimes he didn't seem sure where we were. He was content to just sit around the house. If not for other Vancouver friends who came to spend a couple of weeks with us, we would not have seen any of the medieval castles, visited the bustling outdoor markets that offered delicious cheeses and foie gras, or toured any of the local wineries, sampling their excellent vintages.

Another time, we were invited to accompany one of the senior members of our church to her time-share in Maui. Being close to ninety, she was not able to make her annual trip alone anymore. All we had to do was be company for her—certainly no problem, since we knew her well and enjoyed being with her. What a fabulous opportunity! But when we got to Maui, Bill wouldn't leave the suite unless dragged out. He didn't want to come with me for romantic walks on the beach, either in the early morning or at night. He just sat on the couch watching television, and his behaviour made me furious. What a waste of tropical sunsets and full moons. Angry and hurt, I swore I would never go on vacation with him again. As it turned out, I didn't. We never went on another trip.

Shortly after that Bill quit his job at the Crane Library, saying he just wanted to concentrate on his acting career. Then he stopped auditioning for speaking parts, having asked his agent to just send him out on background or extra jobs. He said he was tired of going out on cattle calls, competing at auditions with a group of men who all looked alike. "This acting thing is a mug's game," he complained. "Whose turn is it to get one or two lines in the next American production?" Next he started turning down even background jobs and became basically unemployed, just sitting around the apartment doing nothing.

One day it occurred to me that something more than lethargy was going on with Bill. Two good friends of ours had come over to help us install a Murphy bed. Three years before, we had joined the ranks of proud grandparents. Dianne and Mike had presented us with two darling boys, Matthew and Kyle. Eighteen months apart, they were adorable additions to the family and gave me a full to overflowing quota of hugs. Competing for Grandmother of the Year, I regularly invited the boys for hilariously fun sleepovers. The problem was, they quickly outgrew the children's foldout bed I used to set up beside our bed. They needed real beds. We needed another bedroom. We needed to move. So we did. We sold our suite and bought a two-bedroom apartment in the same building. Thus the need for a Murphy bed.

I didn't want to dedicate the spare room entirely to overnight stays, and with a Murphy bed, the room would double as a den or home office. Enter our good friends, tools in hand, to assist. Well, the truth is, they came over to *do* the installation. Neither Bill nor I were at all handy with a hammer or screwdriver. Partway through this project, Bill started to ask what our friends were doing and wondered why we needed a new bed. "Our bed is just fine," he said. At first, we all just laughed off his comments, making a few rude bed jokes, but Bill didn't stop. He kept on about how we didn't need a second bed. He liked the bed we had. Eventually our friends lost patience and barked at him, "Give it a rest, Bill. If you don't want the damned Murphy bed, we'll just go home and you can forget it." At this point I in turn snapped at them, "Leave him alone. He's having a bad day." They finished installing the wretched bed and then left—mad. After that incident, we barely saw them again.

A week later, Bill was the scheduled lector at church. He walked up to the lectern as normal, announced which passages of scripture he would be reading, and started. About one minute in, he went silent and looked absolutely flummoxed. He'd lost his place and didn't know what to do. I walked up to the front, stood beside him, and, recognizing where his reading had stopped, I put my finger on the spot and he continued. Staying there with him, I turned the pages to the next reading and again pointed to where it started. At coffee time after church, a few of our friends gave me a sympathetic nod, and one said, "Well done." I was sad to see another example of Bill's problem (whatever the problem was) come to light, but glad that this glaring incident happened among such supportive friends. I have to admit too that I was also glad to discover I was able to just walk up and take charge. I wondered if "taking charge" would start to be a regular occurrence.

Bill's doctor said he was suffering from anxiety attacks and prescribed an extraordinarily strong drug called Ativan. I'm not sure what the GP thought Ativan would accomplish, but it created no positive results. Bill became depressed and uncommunicative to the point where sometimes he was like a zombie, barely speaking. This was a man who used to talk all the time and always in rich, confident tones. And one night, just after dinner, he started to shake all over—as if he was freezing. But he wasn't cold. Nor was he hot—no fever. Just these terrible shakes. I was really worried and had no idea what was happening. I thought about calling 911 but didn't know what I would tell the operator. "My husband is shaking all over"? So I just put him to bed and hoped for the best.

He slept right through till almost noon the next day and when he got up he was fine, as if nothing had happened. I didn't know if the symptoms were an Ativan reaction or something else, but I did know that something had to be done about Bill's health, and I was sure the drug his doctor had him on was not the answer. I thought that in addition to being depressed, he was also bored: no work, no socializing with friends, no more projects with the strata committees he had been involved with at our condo. And I started to wonder how could I help him—and help us. Maybe a change of pace was needed.

Through this, I was also getting depressed. Some days I didn't want to come home from the office. Why would I? When I got home I would just find Bill hanging around the apartment, having done nothing all day and looking so sad. My evenings and weekends were boring and worrisome. Our social life had completely dried up. One sunny Saturday in September, I really needed to get out. A walk at the beach down on English Bay would be perfect. Or a stroll through Stanley Park. But there was no way I could pry Bill off his chair in the living room. Looking back, I'm embarrassed to say that I lost it that day and had a real hissy fit, shouting at Bill about how boring life had become and what a drag he was, and then stomped out by myself. My walk around the park was not the uplifting stroll I had hoped for, but it was the therapy I needed—a chance to look at our situation calmly and make some decisions.

What I didn't know at that time was that Bill had developed the early stages of dementia. What I *did* know was that the man I had married twenty years before was slipping away, and I didn't know why. Something had to be done. Step one, I decided, was to get him off those wretched pills. During a serious heart-to-heart with his doctor, I explained what was happening, and we started to wean Bill off the Ativan. The doctor decreased the dosage and slowly, over three or four months, I reduced Bill's daily intake. Next step was to figure out what a change of pace would look like. At the time, I had no idea what that would be or that it would be a complete 180-degree shift in lifestyle for both of us.

CHAPTER 3

From the condo to the country

THE PLAN WAS HATCHED ON January 21st, 2008, my sixty-first birthday. Dianne and Mike, along with Matthew and Kyle (still the cutest grandsons in captivity), were visiting for a celebration dinner. It had taken the family over an hour to drive in from Abbotsford, a small city sixty kilometres east of Vancouver, where they lived on a five-acre farm with their six horses, three dogs, and an unknown number of barn cats.

Over dinner, Dianne casually mentioned that the house next door to them was for sale. The first words out of my mouth were "We'll take it." Bill's first words were "We'll what?"

"Never mind. We'll talk," I said and smiled convincingly.

I knew this house well because I had visited Dianne's neighbour a couple of times, and during our first glass of wine there, this neighbour had given me the tour. The two-storey house was newer than many of the others on the street—probably built in the mid-'80s. It had a beautifully landscaped garden and yard and an impressive-looking front gate that, when opened, enabled access to the short driveway and double-car garage. Inside, the large, bright kitchen overlooked the well-groomed backyard, which featured an inviting patio situated beside a pond and a gurgling fountain. Beyond this, the back field stretched as far as the eye could see to the blueberry bushes bordering the property behind. Upstairs, there were two spare bedrooms and a master bedroom more like a master suite, with double doors that opened inwards. It had a fireplace and a separate dressing room adjacent to the bathroom ensuite, with a huge soaker tub big enough for two. Like Dianne and Mike's, the house was set on five acres and came with a barn and hayfield and plenty of space for animals to graze, should one be into that sort of thing. The current owners were not.

Up until that moment, the thought of living in the heart of the Fraser Valley, one of BC's primary agricultural areas, was the farthest thing from my mind. Add in a barn and the possibility of milking cows or some other farmer thing, and my eyes would glaze over. I was still in shock that eight years previously my city-raised daughter and her husband had bought a farm. Every time I thought of Dianne mucking around in a horse stall, I wondered how that had happened.

But the moment I heard about the availability of that house, it was as if I had been hit by lightning. To start with, my grandmotherly hormones began twitching. I could be next door to the boys. I could get hugs every day! The thought of being part of their daily life—and having them part of mine—was irresistible. Plus, they were the only immediate family Bill and I had, cousins notwithstanding. We had always had a close relationship with Dianne and Mike, so the wild idea of becoming farmers and neighbours of theirs suddenly looked much more civilized.

In the blink of an eye, city life became uninteresting. And our apartment felt like a cage. Visions of green fields with horses grazing in the sunshine started to dance before my eyes. Dianne and I spent the rest of the evening fantasizing about the move. Enthusiastically getting behind the idea, she assured me that she and Mike would do all the farm work on our place as well as on their own. They would take down the fencing between our two properties and run her horses across both sets of fields. They would teach us what we needed to know about rural living. It would be terrific. During all this excited glee, Bill and Mike wandered away to calmer corners of the apartment, Mike no doubt reassuring Bill that this off-the-wall idea would be forgotten by the next day. They probably thought my sudden enthusiasm about such a drastic lifestyle change might have been influenced by the glasses of Chardonnay I'd been enjoying during my birthday celebration. Or that the concept of being near lively family members—witness the two boys roaring around our living room—had caused me to become temporarily delusional. But they were wrong. I was totally in.

Even the next day, when the empty wine bottles were lined up in military fashion on the counter, I was sure that buying the property next door to Dianne and Mike would solve our problems. Adopting a completely new lifestyle would be a wonderful adventure, I told myself. I was sure the move would be good for Bill; country living would be exciting, definitely not boring, and we would be the talk of all our friends. I loved the house and envisioned us sitting on the patio summer evenings with a glass of something delicious, admiring the horses as they frolicked in the back field. I would plan barbecues with our city friends, who would come out for the weekend. Our apartment faced north, which made it dark, and I wondered whether the low light might be adding to Bill's depression. The house in Abbotsford was anything but dark. The complete change of routine would be good for him, and he might enjoy being close to the family. This was a good opportunity to get to know the boys better. Deep down, I was also sure that the family would offer me more than just how-to-farm help. They would be there for me when I needed help for Bill, whatever that help would turn out to be.

Become farmers? Bill took a bit of convincing. Leaving Vancouver and moving out to a farm did not strike him as a brilliant idea. But he eventually came around. I was up front with him and said that I was worried about his health. I didn't come right out and say his mental health, but that's what I meant. Physically he was just fine—no heart or blood pressure issues that one might expect in a man in his mid-seventies, and he had no mobility concerns. But while he had perked up a bit since being off the Ativan, often he was still down, and there were times when he seemed confused or anxious. He was the chairperson for an annual ACTRA awards luncheon, but a year before my fateful birthday dinner, he had a really tough time focusing on the preparation. And a few months before that, he was asked to take over the narration for the River City Gospel Jazz group he belonged to because Alan Reynolds, the leader, was sick—a job that normally would have come easily to him. That day he was unusually nervous or agitated.

For some unknown reason, I was really excited at the thought of living on a farm. No idea where that came from—maybe a throwback from some agrarian ancestor. Bill said he understood my desire for a change and said he was sorry he'd become such a drag. My pact with him was that if he absolutely hated our new situation after a year, we would sell and move back to town. I really loved him, and I was sorry that our life plans had taken such a downturn, that our expectation for a continued good time in Vancouver had been upended.

In my early sixties, when I was starting to think about what retirement would look like, I had expected that when I was ready to pack in the nine-to-five routine, I would keep pounding away on my home office computer a couple of days a week. I would work freelance, as I had in the past, offering my PR experience to small clients, possibly writing slice-of-life magazine articles, and maybe developing websites for start-ups, should I be able to remember the HTML code I had learned in a course at BCIT. In addition, I had expected that Bill and I would spend lots of time socializing with our friends; would travel a bit, and would generally enjoy ourselves in the coming years. We didn't have specific plans for the next stage of our life. I just assumed we would go with the flow and spend more time doing what we liked, without a job getting in the way. But now that the opportunity had materialized, I was convinced that this move to Abbotsford was a good idea.

Before hiring a realtor and signing on the dotted line to seal this venture, I needed to be sure that Dianne and Mike were really okay with having us so close. You know, boundaries and all that. My primary concern was Mike, who would have his mother-in-law living within spying distance. So I asked him specifically, and in private, whether he had any concerns. I gave him a huge opportunity to be honest, but his comment was, "It will be great having you so close. This way when you want me to come over to fix your computer, I won't have to drive for an hour to get there." Did I mention Mike is really easygoing and has a great sense of humour?

In spite of my concerns, or maybe because of them, Dianne and Mike were totally supportive of our move. In exchange for free babysitting, they promised to teach us everything we needed to know about being farmers. The truth was, what Bill and I knew about country living would not fill three lines in a kid's scribbler. We had both been raised in the city and had primarily lived in apartments all our lives. Except for when he was a kid in his parents' home, Bill had never even pushed a lawn mower. So all we knew about farm life was what we had noticed when we visited Mike and Dianne. And often that was just the bad smell that permeated the air early each spring. Yuck. Besides lacking farm cred, as I've said, neither of us were handy. Our idea of getting something fixed was to call the building manager. But all that notwithstanding, Dianne and Mike were the ones who cracked the first bottle of champagne when the deal was signed.

In fact, that did not happen for six more months, and we ended up buying a *different* house and farm, farther down the street. We discovered in our dealings that the owners of the house next door were not, as realtors like to say, motivated vendors. For reasons of their own, their house was on and off the market all spring. We waited. We made offers, we amended offers. Our realtor, bless his soul, even travelled from Vancouver to Abbotsford to meet with their realtor, hoping to close the deal. All to no avail. They weren't selling.

In the midst of all this backing and forthing, another of Mike and Dianne's neighbours put their farm on the market. This place, also on five acres, across the street and two houses down, was not as "glamorous" as the first house, but it had promise. The kitchen and bathrooms needed serious updating, but nothing that a creative interior designer and a pot of money couldn't fix. A split level built in the mid-'70s, the house had three bedrooms up and a wraparound deck off the kitchen that looked north over the fields and barn. On the lower level, half the basement comprised a fully finished family room with fireplace, tasteful carpeting, and sliding doors out to the backyard. In the other half was a bright and airy one-bedroom mother-in-law suite that the current owners had built for one of their relatives.

Our new home sweet home

From the street, the house was quite pretty. A graceful weeping willow tree stood beside the gravel driveway that led to the two-car carport. A white picket fence ran the width of the front lawn, from the driveway over to the beginning of the side field. Most of the property was behind the house, where fields stretched from the back of the barn to a wooded area in the distance. To the right of the backyard was a stretch of six-foot-high cedar fence panels that separated the "people's area" from the horses' side fields. Additionally, a stream divided the property from its easterly neighbour and then meandered across the back end of the acreage, going on to cross behind three neighbouring farms to the west.

After three months of fantasizing about A-frame barns in the backyard and fields of hay, it was now time to get practical. This farm was in fact a better buy than the one next door to Mike and Dianne. The asking price was less and the downstairs suite promised to be a source of income. How could we finance this outrageous idea? Selling the condo was obviously the first thing to do. Negotiating a mortgage came next. Of course, our friends thought we were crazy—and not just because we seemed intent on remaking the 1960s TV sitcom *Green Acres*, with me playing the Eva Gabor character and Bill subbing for Eddie Albert. Those who knew also questioned our sanity because we would have to take on a mortgage—considered unwise at our ages. After all, thanks to luck and family circumstances, we had been mortgage-free since we had purchased our Vancouver condo sixteen years before.

Now here we were, sitting in the office of our financial adviser, asking how we could take on debt when most couples would be saving for retirement. Selling the apartment was easy. We got a good price but we were still short of the asking price for the farm. Believe it or not, in 2008, it was possible to take out a forty-year mortgage, which at our age was ridiculous. Instead, with the help of an experienced mortgage broker, we negotiated a line of credit that both covered the shortfall between the selling price of the condo and the purchase price of the farm *and* gave us access to some additional cash. The rental income from the suite downstairs covered the interest payments on the line of credit, so we were, in effect, still living "mortgage free."

* * *

Although I had considered all contingencies, moving day—August 30, 2008—was fraught with a fair amount of confusion and angst. The moving company I had hired sent the wrong-size truck and the movers couldn't get all our stuff in. They didn't have another truck to send on short notice and said we would have to rent one from the local U-Haul. Thank heavens for our great friends Ben and Evy, who lived upstairs, and Phyllis from next door, who had come to the apartment to see if we needed any help. Ben went with Bill to rent the extra truck, and Evy and Phyllis stayed with me to help direct traffic in the suite.

Finally we were on our way. Waving goodbye to Phyllis, and giving directions to Ben, who had volunteered to drive the extra truck, Bill and I each got into our own vehicles and led the convoy east on Highway 1 for the hour-long excursion to country living. Ten minutes from our new life, we cut off the highway and entered another world. The country roads leading to our place were lined with fields of golden hay waiting to be cut. Neat farmhouses nestled behind white fences. Signs in front of some places advertised farm-fresh eggs, $3.00. There wasn't a high-rise in sight, and the only traffic we saw consisted of two cars and one giant flat deck truck hauling what looked like giant marshmallows. (These, we learned later, were round bales of hay—our farming lessons had started.) Our house, along with nine others, was located on a quiet cul-de-sac about a kilometre long, with minimal traffic other than the neighbours' comings and goings. Mike and Dianne lived in the second house on the left. Ours was the fifth house on the right.

One of my favourite memories from moving day was the moment we turned into our street. Bill and I manoeuvred our cars side by side and just sat there for a minute, each gazing down the road towards "home," each momentarily lost in our own thoughts. Mine were, *I sure hope this works.* Bill's were a mystery to me. Our street had no sidewalks, just grassy ditches in front of each property. No streetlights either that I could see. The sun had just set and dusk was falling. It was starting to get chilly. Giving each other the nod, Bill and I drove the last quarter-mile and entered our driveway totally together—joined at the hubcaps, as it were, a symbolic harbinger of our future life. Before getting out of our cars, we looked over at each other, smiled and nodded, then headed inside hand in hand.

We were greeted at our front door by Dianne and Mike and Mike's mom, Carol, who was visiting from out of town. They were waiting to welcome us with a slow cooker full of delicious stew and a few bottles of red wine. The boys, at five and six, were running around the empty rooms, excitedly waiting for Nanny and Grampa Bill to arrive. It had been a long day and we were awfully glad to see the movers unloading our stuff. To make way for the much-needed renovations on the main floor, we moved into the basement suite on day one. So I pointed the movers down the stairs with our immediate needs—the bed, chesterfield, and chairs, kitchen boxes, and so on—and up the stairs with everything else. Ben and Evy stayed for some of the stew and the grand tour, then headed back to the city to return the rented truck.

The previous owners had installed laminate flooring throughout the house and built the basement suite. Other than that, they had retained the thirty-year-old decor, which included green and pink fixtures in the bathrooms and rooster wallpaper in the kitchen. These would have to go. As for the outbuildings, according to Dianne, who knew much more than we did about these things, the barn on the property was in excellent shape. Built at the end of the backyard, in full view from the wraparound deck, the red A-frame structure looked like it belonged on a movie set. Its big sliding front door opened onto a long corridor called a shed row, I learned, with two horse stalls on one side and one on the other. A side door at the back opened out to the side fields, where the horses would graze.

This barn excited Dianne because she wanted to move two of her horses over. She was into breeding horses and needed more barn space. The barn also had a hayloft, complete with wooden ladder that reminded me of the movie *Heidi* I had seen as a kid. The ladder led straight up from the ground floor to a hinged trapdoor that you had to push back and crawl through to get to the barn's upper floor. Over time I got good at doing that. Just past the horses' stalls was a fully operational chicken coop with roosts, nesting boxes, and a little door to give the chickens access to their own fenced-off field. Hooray! Farm-fresh eggs, here we come.

The day we moved in was a Saturday. On Sunday morning, after a great first night's sleep in the downstairs bedroom, I crept quietly out of bed. Leaving Bill still snuggled under the covers, I made a pot of coffee and wandered up the stairs to the main floor. Standing in the empty kitchen, coffee cup in hand, I found myself gazing out over the back deck in absolute awe, first at the presence of a barn at the official end of the backyard (who has a barn in their backyard?), and then at the expanse of property that stretched straight back behind the barn to the woods in the distance. This amazing place was now home! Barn and all.

Wandering to the front of the house, I picked my way through the living room's clutter of furniture and boxes, which were stashed all over while we set up house, for the time being, in the basement. I ended up standing at the large picture window, admiring the lawn and thinking that we should paint the front fence. Soon Bill joined me and together we walked through the house, just looking and smiling. It felt good—cluttered but good.

An hour or so later, I heard a vehicle rumbling up our gravel driveway and, looking out, saw our next-door neighbour, Gerry, arriving in his John Deere Gator, his darling little dog Buttons sitting on the passenger seat. I knew Gerry from visits we had made to Dianne and Mike's in the past. What I didn't know was that Gerry had very bad knees and trundled around the neighbourhood in his UTV, usually accompanied by Buttons. When I answered the door that day, I was reminded of the time, eight years earlier, that I had answered the door on day two of Dianne and Mike's farm adventure. In addition to welcoming them, their next-door neighbour Terry had wanted to fill them in on the ins and outs of retaining their property's farm status for tax purposes. For years he had been grazing a few of his cattle on the land now owned by Mike and Dianne. This gave him enough food for his small herd and had enabled the previous owners to claim farm status. Were Mike and Dianne in favour of this arrangement too? Before long, the deal was done. The neighbouring cows could stay. If I recall correctly, the agreement was reached even before the first brew Mike had offered Terry was popped open. Newbie hospitality is always a good start to neighbour relations.

Now here I was again opening the door to a next-door neighbour, who had come to welcome *us* to the street, chuckle with us at our sense of adventure, and offer any help we might need in adjusting to rural living. I invited Gerry in, but he was not crazy about tackling the stairs up or down so we talked at the front door. "I just wanted to say I'm next door if you need anything. Those cows you see on the other side of the fence are mine. Don't let the bull scare you. He's big but not interested in people." *Okay*

Over the years, Gerry and his wife, Rose, would be warm, dependable neighbours and friends. They would also be a font of knowledge about our house, since they had lived on the adjacent property for over three decades. Their practical information came in handy many times. For instance, one day the septic tank overflowed and backed up into the downstairs bathroom. First we ran down the street to Dianne's to find out who to call. Then, when the service guys arrived to pump out the system, we had to dash over to Gerry's, because there was no sign of the access to the septic tank. We knew the tank itself was underground in the backyard, but access is usually marked by the lid to the tank or by something sticking up out of the ground (a dead giveaway, one would think). Ours had neither indicator.

When called upon for help, Gerry drove over, parked his UTV in the driveway, and slowly made his way into our backyard like this was an everyday occurrence. For a few minutes he stood looking up at the three bathroom windows, two on the main floor and one in the basement. He paced back and forth a bit, and then he pointed to the ground. "Dig here," he said. Sure enough, the cover to the septic tank was right there, about six feet beneath the lawn. After the guys from Ace Tank Services had finished emptying the tank, they raised the access to the tank and installed a new lid that was noticeable and flush with the grass. "For next time," they said. Gee, I could hardly wait. While the technicians were doing their magic, I was doing mine—in the basement bathroom. Some days being a farmer is not very glamorous.

Kyle and Matty's first day of school

On the third morning of our new life, I got to run down the street to see Matthew and Kyle off to their first day of school: Matty entering grade one, Kyle starting kindergarten. They attended King Traditional Elementary, which meant they wore uniforms. With excited smiles on their faces, they stood on the steps of their house for Nanny's photo op, all scrubbed and shiny in their official navy-blue shorts, white shirts, and pristine—but not for long—running shoes. Each of them carried a new lunch box—Spider-Man for Kyle and Star Wars for Matty. Being there in person, I had such a lump in my throat that I could hardly get the words out to wish them a great first day of school. My first real "nanny thing" was as special as I had imagined.

* * *

One week to the day after we'd moved in, it was Bill's seventy-eighth birthday, and I could hardly wait to invite all our friends from our former life to help him celebrate. Among the two dozen enthusiastic well-wishers were Ben and Evy, who came, partly I'm sure, to see if we had been able to get all the furniture into the house, and Elaine and John, our long-time friends from Gabriola Island, off the coast of Vancouver Island. Elaine and I had been friends, seeing each other through thick and thin, for almost fifty years. We were there for one divorce and one remarriage each; the arrival of one new baby—mine; two moves each across the country between Vancouver and Toronto; hours of phone calls; and gallons of wine to celebrate, commiserate, advise, and share life-altering tips.

I suspected that while our friends did indeed want to wish Bill a happy day, they really came to see with their own eyes what we had done. When I had told them that Bill and I were going to buy a farm in Abbotsford, everyone had burst out laughing, including my work colleagues. As I said, they thought we were crazy and had plenty of questions. "What about the commute? Won't you miss going to shows or seeing your friends? What if you get snowed in? What do you know about farming?" Arriving on the day of the party, they found us living out of boxes in the basement suite with limited kitchenware and minimal furniture, waiting for the interior designer and tradesmen to transform the upstairs from retro to contemporary.

Whenever I think of Bill's birthdays, I always smile. Partly because those celebrations were such an integral part of the fun we had during our marriage, and partly because Bill managed to change our tried-and-true family tradition of how to celebrate birthdays. He insisted birthdays be celebrated on *the day*. For years our family had been celebrating birthdays whenever it was convenient—the weekend before, the day after, anytime at all. For us, birthdays could and should be celebrated more than once. Parties could be dragged out for days and days—sometimes from one weekend to the next. While going along with this concept, Bill still made sure that a celebration also happened on *the day*. And not just for him. For us too. This requirement was easy for Bill because in most years, his birthday fell on the Labour Day long weekend. Over the years, Bill's birthday was always a great excuse for a party. And I loved throwing surprise parties for him. I'm sure eventually he wasn't really surprised, but being the great thespian that he was, he did the "Oh, no" thing convincingly well.

The first time I tried this, we were still "new" as a couple and I had not yet met most of his friends. My comedy-writer cousin Sandy, who by coincidence had been one of the writers on *Dr. Bundolo*, knew enough of Bill's friends to give me phone numbers and get the guest list started. Calling up "strangers" and trotting out my well-worn line "You don't know me but," I invited them to a surprise fifty-second birthday party for Bill. To my surprise, they all came. Turns out they had all heard that Bill was seeing someone, and they were curious to meet me. Sandy and his wife, Mary Anne, let everyone in while I took Bill out to dinner and then invited him back—nudge nudge, wink wink. When we walked into my place and Bill saw everyone there, he was speechless, which is saying something for him. The party was a great success and I was excited to meet his interesting friends. Some, like weather forecaster Norm Grohmann, I had been watching on TV for years.

Then there was the roast we had for Bill's sixtieth at the home of our great friends Bob and Marge Sibson in New Westminster. Bob had been a singer-dancer in the early days of CBC Television, a stage actor with Theatre Under the Stars, and the soloist at our wedding. Marge had been a professional dancer with the Royal Winnipeg Ballet. They lived in a charming heritage house that boasted, along with its leaded windows and turn-of-the-century architecture, a basement large enough to accommodate ten 50-gallon carboys of fermenting wine. As a group, we all enthusiastically pitched in every autumn to support their winemaking as soon as the grapes arrived. I was never sure if Bill was really surprised when Bob and Marge's front door was thrown open to reveal a group of keen friends who, I suspect, had been into one or two rounds from last year's basement vintage before we got there. But the evening held a surprise for me.

While these friends, many of whom were performers who loved to be centre stage, were sharing their funny stories about Bill's past, I learned he had a penchant for dropping his trousers in public. This act started during one of the *Dr. Bundolo* live-to-tape shows at UBC's Student Union Building, where the onstage humour and ad lib gags perfectly suited the audience, which was mostly engineering students. In the middle of one of the sketches, in a move that had nothing to do with the script, Bill unzipped, dropped his pants to the floor, and flashed his striped drawers. The audience went crazy, hooting and hollering. Don Kowalchuk, the show's producer, went a little crazy too. His job was to edit the live shenanigans that took place every week into something suitable for radio's general audience, cutting out actions that didn't translate well to audio only.

The best party, though, was the "This Is Your Life, Bill Buck" bus tour for his sixty-fifth. Bill always bragged about being born and raised in Vancouver and told anyone who would listen, mostly me, about every house he had ever lived in and every school he had ever attended, including the names of his favourite teachers. Based on these stories, I organized a surprise bus tour. About twenty-five guests piled into a full-size Greyhound bus, with wine and cheese on offer and a convenient on-board washroom. As the tour got underway, everyone aboard relived Bill's life as a true born-here Vancouverite. Starting at St. Paul's Hospital, where *he* started, we toured past the houses he had lived in and the places he had worked. My plan was that the bus driver, Jeff, a professional tour operator for Greyhound and a long-time friend from my Vancouver AM days, would read the script I had written, starting his spiel with "And on your left is the hospital where Bill Buck was born." Later he was to say, "On your right is the first house Bill lived in," and so on. But the moment Bill got onto the bus, having fallen for my ruse of meeting the driver for a quick coffee, he twigged as to what was happening, took over the mic, and did his own spiel. All Jeff had to do was follow the route I had given him. That was a challenge in itself, because Bill had been raised on Vancouver's east side, which has some very narrow streets. Manoeuvring that giant bus around some of those corners was a job that only a very experienced driver could accomplish.

At each landmark we stopped, pushed Bill out of the bus, and made him hold up a sign I had had made for the photo op. In front of his elementary school, the sign read, "Bill Buck slept here." In front of one of the parks, the sign read, "Bill Buck lost it here." But the most hilarious moment was when the bus stopped in front of one house where Bill had lived. As the door opened, we all saw the current owner pop up from her knees, where she had been working in her garden, and stare in wonder at the bus. Quick as I could, I jumped out and said to her, "Bill Buck used to live here." Everyone in the bus cracked up in hysterics and the mystified woman just said, "Oh." On the way through downtown Vancouver, the bus pulled over on Georgia Street in front of the CBC building to let the *Dr. Bundolo* group out. And, you guessed it, Bill chose that moment to drop his pants in the middle of the intersection. The others huddled around his indecency and ushered him back into the bus for another glass of wine. At that point we decided to head back to the apartment before we all got arrested.

An apt cake for Bill's seventy-seventh birthday

Bill's first birthday celebration on the farm—September 7, 2008—was another memorable birthday for us all. The day dawned warm and sunny, and the party was set up in the backyard. Mike came over early to mow the lawn, and Dianne and Mike then brought over extra lawn furniture and lots of buckets of ice for the drinks. For a housewarming gift they had given us a new barbecue, complete with rotisserie. This we christened at the party, serving burgers and hot dogs along with plenty of appies, drinks, and a delicious cake. All the guests toured the house and gave their opinions about what changes we should make to the kitchen. Poring over the flooring samples I had set out was the parlour game du jour. Bill was in his element, and he loved showing everyone around. He even smiled broadly when the guests admired the horses standing like amazing lawn ornaments nearby.

"Are they really yours?" they asked.

"Yes," bragged Bill.

"Wow!" they said. Then they all went home muttering, "They really did It!" But before leaving, they placed their orders for our first collection of farm-fresh eggs.

Yup, we did it

CHAPTER 4

Farmer wannabes

OUR COUNTRY-LIVING LEARNING CURVE CLIMBED almost hourly for the first couple of months. I had taken two weeks' vacation for the move and the adjustment period, thinking naively that fourteen days would be adequate. On about day four, when Bill and I went out to the end of the driveway to get our mail and newspaper, we discovered that our mailbox had fallen off its post overnight. "Must have been windy last night," we concluded wisely to each other. Like the condo dwellers we still were, we said to each other, "Hmm. I wonder who we call at the post office to get a new one?" Then we trotted down the street to ask Dianne. After she stopped laughing, she handed us a hammer and said, "Welcome to the country." No surprise, it was Mike who came over after work to put our mailbox back together.

We also needed lessons in taking out the garbage, now that we no longer had a garburator or apartment-building garbage chute. The garbage truck came once a week to collect recyclables, which had to be put in just the right kind of blue see-through plastic bag. Every other week, the same truck also collected the real trash bag, which wasn't supposed to be very full because we all had a compost pile. Yeah. Right. Working on that.

After we'd had a week of cultural adjustment, a man we'd never seen before arrived on a tractor and announced we were going to be hayed. Back down the street we went for elucidation. "Hayed? Not a problem," said Dianne. "Ray does all the work." She explained that he drives a mower that cuts down the hay in the field. Then he returns three or four more times to fluff it up. (That's called tedding the hay and it's done in advance of baling.) After that, he's back again, with a different machine, this time to bale the hay. For a greenhorn, the process was fascinating to watch. When the time came, the "fluffed up" hay went in one end of the baler Ray was driving, and square bundles popped out the back. In no time at all, our field was covered in tidy rows of hay cubes. Then it was our turn to work.

The day our hay was baled, Dianne, Mike, and the boys arrived at our place right after Mike got off work. With their flatbed trailer hitched to their pickup truck, we worked to retrieve the bales and move them to the barn. Bill drove the truck, while the boys rode in the back. Meanwhile we three heaved the bales, all 130 of them, onto the deck of the trailer. Since each weighed about fifty pounds, I was grateful that the personal trainer I had had in town had helped me develop decent biceps. The job had to be done in short order because the bales could not be left on the field overnight. Dew (or worse, rain) is bad for the hay. Once off the field, the bales were stored for winter—some in our hayloft and some in Mike and Diane's barn, to augment the hay that had been taken off their field the day before.

Hay! Aren't we getting good?

Up until that moment, it had never occurred to me to wonder how hay gets up to a hayloft. Enter the neighbour from across the street, who loaned us his hay elevator. Looking not unlike any shopping centre escalator, this contraption is basically a conveyor belt that leans against the barn wall. When it's plugged in, its pulley system carries the bales from the ground up to the hayloft. Bill and I stood at the bottom, putting the bales onto the elevator from the flat deck. Mike and Dianne worked in the loft, pulling the bales off and stacking them into position. During this procedure, the boys ran around the yard, playing in the stray piles of hay that were scattered about. Since their barn did not have a hayloft, they were excited to get up into ours to make forts, but their parents held them back until the work was done. For the next few years, on many afternoons my heart would jump for joy as I looked out the kitchen window towards the barn and saw two blond heads cavorting in the hayloft. Sometimes there were more than two heads, as their friends got wind of this great place to play.

The best part of haying, besides the beer we drank after, was when I got to climb into the hayloft myself and throw a week's worth of bales down to the lower-level storage area for the horses. I was really catching on to this farmer thing. Yes, the horses were now in residence! Midweek after our move, Dianne and Mike had come clip-clopping down the street, each leading a horse. The older and taller one, Sassy, a glossy chestnut, was Dianne's off-the-track thoroughbred. Sassy had been Dianne's primary riding horse since before the boys were born, but at nineteen, she was pretty much retired. The other horse was Cassidy, a ten-year-old pony who had been at Dianne and Mike's for many years too. Cassidy used to get hitched up to a buggy, as in horse and buggy, and be driven around the property just for fun. He was past that when he came to our place, but he was still lively and loved to chase around the field with Sassy. Turning into our front yard, Dianne and Mike led the horses down the side driveway, across our backyard, through the barn, and out the side door to the field. We had wanted them there for Bill's birthday party, to dazzle our city friends, and Dianne was glad to accommodate us.

I was excited to welcome the horses because they looked so picturesque grazing in the field and because I've always loved horses, even though I didn't ride. Or, at least, hadn't ridden since I was a kid at summer camp. Except for that one Christmas Day six years before when Dianne was largely pregnant with Matthew. Bill and I were there for the weekend and after we'd all opened our gifts, Dianne said she wanted to go for a ride. It was one of those sunny cold winter days that invite outside activities. However, none of us were keen on Dianne going out alone, so I offered to tag along on one of their other horses. I must admit I was pretty nervous but told myself this would be just like riding a bicycle. Once you've done it, you never forget. Bill was nervous too. I heard he worried the whole time we were gone. Would I fall off? Would the horses bolt? Would Dianne go into labour? Bill was a natural worrier, and I guess this ride idea fed right into his anxiety. Dianne and I did not go far but the jaunt was fun—and definitely the last time I chose to climb onto a horse's back. My leg muscles were stiff for a whole week.

Meet Sassy. Isn't she gorgeous?

Knowing we were going to house Dianne's horses, I insisted on a couple of ground rules. I was happy to feed Sassy and Cassidy and let them in and out as needed. I loved throwing the hay down and got good at checking their water and spoiling them with hand-held treats. I also loved brushing Sassy—not Cassidy, that wasn't his thing—and watching when the farrier came to trim and shape the horses' hooves. Starting with the front hooves, the farrier turned her back to the horse, bent over so her behind was bumping into the horse's chest, picked up a leg, and braced it between her knees. Then she started the equine pedicure. I knew that horses needed to have their hooves tended to, but it was a real eye-opener to see how it was done. So, although I would help with the horses, I made it clear that my job was *not* to shovel out the stalls. (I do have my limits, you know.) Dianne was happy to come over every morning to do that, and often we would have coffee after.

After haying and horse-tending, keeping chickens came next on the learn-to-do list. I had been pining for farm-fresh eggs and could hardly wait to fill the coop. Once we were a bit more settled, at 9:00 one Monday morning, right after dropping off the boys at school, Bill, Dianne, and I loaded into the back of their pickup the three large wire cages Dianne had borrowed from a friend, and we headed off to Echo Hatchery and Poultry Farm to buy fifty egg-laying chickens. I didn't know anything about the different breeds of chickens, but I had heard of Rhode Island Reds. When I asked if that's what we were getting, Dianne said no, they were too expensive. Instead we purchased brown laying hens, although their feathers had a lot of red in them. They cost about seven dollars each, if my memory serves.

At Echo, after we paid the bill, we drove around to the back door of the hatchery, at which point I went into shock. The young lad who worked there slid open the door and started bringing out the chickens, hanging upside down, flapping their wings frantically and squawking loudly as he gripped them by their feet. Since he was only able to carry two or three in each hand at a time, he had to make a few trips to bring out all fifty hens. Our job was to manage the cage doors, opening and then quickly closing them to keep the chickens from flying away. I don't know what I was expecting, but this wasn't it. I guess I thought the chickens would be carried gently to the truck in someone's arms. But real life on the farm ain't always pretty.

The racket the birds made all the way home was deafening, and when we got them back to the farm, our work had just begun. Each bird had to have her wings clipped so she wouldn't fly away. *What?* Mike's uncle Ted, whose farm was a few miles away, had given Dianne instructions on how to do this. Having chickens was new to Dianne and Mike too. According to Ted, the procedure would be exceedingly messy but simple, and painless for the chickens (in spite of all the ear-piercing screeching they did during the process). And it would take a team of three to do each bird. We learned that it was not necessary to clip both wings; one side was enough to keep the hens earthbound. "One person"—that would be Dianne—"holds the chicken under one arm and with their other hand spreads out the wing feathers like a fan," Ted had said. "Then the other person"—that would be me—"trims the feathers so they're short."

Bill, being the third person, then carries the clipped bird into the chicken coop and lets her get acquainted with her new home, dipping her beak into the self-watering station and then steering her towards the little side door that leads out to fresh grass and great-tasting bugs. By the time we had finished clipping fifty sets of wing feathers, we were all covered in chicken poop and reeking like, well, like a trio of chicken farmers. But our work was not over yet. We still had to clean out the truck, which by then also smelled like a chicken farm and looked disgusting. Afterwards, the shower in our little basement suite was never more inviting. And our future breakfasts never tasted better.

In addition to loving the eggs they produced, we all got quite attached to the chickens themselves. They were so cute to watch, pecking around in their yard and coming and going through their little door. We also got quite conversant with the various breeds of domestic chickens. We never did buy Rhode Island Reds, but one day when he was searching online, Mike discovered Araucanas, a breed from Chile that lay green eggs. We had to have some—just a few. They were expensive, but the novelty of a green egg in a carton of brown ones was totally worth the price. Then Mike discovered Silkies, or Chinese silk chickens. These are fluffy white chickens that don't lay eggs. They just look pretty strutting around with the flock. Soon we had some of them too.

Everything was humming along in the coop with the various birds until someone told us we should have a rooster. We didn't know why we should have one because we weren't planning on hatching eggs, so we didn't need them to be fertilized. But we got one anyway. Big mistake. The chickens didn't like him, and we discovered where the adjective "henpecked" came from. In no time, that poor guy looked terrible: he had no tail feathers left, and instead of strutting around the yard like he ruled the roost, he slunk around. We soon gave him away to a different farm where he would not be picked on. Another farm lesson learned by doing.

CHAPTER 5

Golden days

HAVING COMPLETED THE VACATION WEEKS I had taken off for the move, it was time for me to return to my job in the city four days a week. Suddenly an early morning commute and new routine became a reality. Every workday, I needed to get the chickens and horses up and out before I started my trek to the office. Even though Bill seemed to be enjoying our new country life, he was not up for clomping around in the barn. But for me the novelty was fun. So early mornings went like this: I would get up around 6:00 a.m., plug in the coffee maker, shower, grab a bite to eat, and dress in my city-girl office clothes. Then I would step into my newly acquired gumboots, making sure the designer pants were safely tucked in, throw on a long and old coat, and head outside. With cooler overnight temperatures now foretelling the start of fall, I would first go to the carport to warm up the eight-year-old BMW I had purchased before thoughts of becoming a farmer ever saw the light of day. Then it was off to the barn, to let out the horses.

Just inside the big sliding barn door sat the little pile of special horse treats that I had put out the night before. After picking them up, I walked down the shed row to Sassy's stall and gave her a few along with a quick snuggle, patting her neck and mane. Enjoying her whinny, I moved across to Cassidy with the remainder of the treats. Next, I opened the side door leading to the fields. I gathered up two armloads of the hay that I had previously tossed down to the spare stall from the loft and threw them into the outside feeders. Breakfast for the horses. They would munch on grass in the field for the rest of the day before being brought in for "dinner" and the night.

Sassy and Cassidy just horsin' around

Letting Sassy and Cassidy out required careful staging that Dianne had taught me. Their stall doors had to be opened in the right order. "Don't open the horses' stall doors before opening the big side door," she had cautioned, "or you will have a barn full of horses dashing around trying to get out." *Got that.* "And don't open the stall doors in the wrong order." *Check.* Being the "boss" of the barn, Sassy had to be let out first. If I opened Cassidy's stall door first and then Sassy's, Sassy would chase Cassidy around the shed row until he went back into his stall so she could be let out first. These two were just like kids. So the routine was: after opening the outside door and tossing out the breakfast hay, I was to open Sassy's door, and after she'd run out, open Cassidy's door. I was on it.

Come and get it

Next to the chicken coop. No sense looking for eggs this early. Bill did that in the afternoons. What I did was refill the hens' feeders with the special poultry crumble we gave them to ensure a balanced diet, check their supply of oyster shell (the calcium mix that helped strengthen their shells), and ensure the automatic watering system was functioning. Then I stood back for the fun part. After opening their outside door, I delighted in watching their antics as they scrambled through it—kind of like watching the traffic from West Vancouver merging from four lanes into two to get onto the Lions Gate Bridge. Except the chickens were not as orderly. Their small door allowed only one chicken at a time through. Each bird pecked and pushed her way towards the opening, squawking, wings a-flapping, determined to get out ahead of the others to feast on a breakfast of bugs and grass.

By 7:30 a.m., the barn family taken care of, it was time I returned to the house: a quick wardrobe change—barn coat and gumboots off, pumps and suit jacket on—a quiet kiss to Bill, who was usually still asleep, and I was ready to hit the highway. The commute from Abbotsford to my job at the Kidney Foundation in Burnaby would have been 45 minutes if I'd had the road to myself. But with rush hour traffic, the trip took more than an hour each way and sometimes longer. The new Port Mann Bridge was under construction, so all of us "Valley People" sat in the Highway 1 "parking lot" for many minutes each way, funnelling onto the old bridge through a labyrinth of weekly lane changes.

But I'm not really complaining, because I did not find my commute a problem. The car was warm and dry, with a working radio and CD player, so as long as I remembered to go to the bathroom before I left, I could just sit back and relax. To offset the boredom or to stay calm—perhaps a bit of both—I listened to books on tape borrowed from the library. Every morning, after checking out the CBC hourly news and weather and taking in an interview or two, so I could sound up to date at the office water cooler, I popped the latest whodunit into my CD player and settled back for an hour of entertainment. The books only became frustrating when I pulled into my parking spot at work just short of the story's end and had to wait till 5:00 p.m. to find out who actually *did* do it. My working days were longer than they had been before, but living in the valley was worth it. I loved the feeling of peace that came over me in the early morning, driving through quiet streets with the mist still on the fields. In the first few weeks, I spent the drive home looking forward to getting back to the farm, to enjoy one of the spectacular sunsets over our back field. Living on the farm was like living in the best of both worlds: all citified in professional garb from nine to five, then jumping into jeans and clogs or boots at night.

For the most part Bill was doing well in our new digs. But sometimes not. At first he seemed fine every night when I got home. While I was at work, he shopped for anything we needed, which he loved to do, and he visited with Dianne. Sometimes she'd drop in for coffee after finishing the barn chores; sometimes he'd mosey down the street to her place. And once a week, the two of them made an event out of a trip to Otter Co-op, a member-owned retail outlet that sells animal feed and supplies plus groceries and household items. There they bought the food we needed for the chickens and large bags of cedar shavings to cover the floor of the coop. After shopping, they would check out the store's lunch counter to see what that day's special was. The two of them had always been close, right from the early days of Bill's visits in North Van. Dianne had been part of our wedding party as a bridesmaid, and Bill had given her away at her own wedding. Now, all these years later, living down the street from each other was working out well for them both.

Midafternoon, Bill would collect the eggs from the chicken coop in the barn. He thought this task was all right so long as he didn't have to scoop out an egg from under a brooding hen. Those eggs got left for me to retrieve when I came home. It surprised me to learn that egg production is cyclical. After we brought the first flock of hens home, they did not start laying right away. It turns out that most hens will lay their first egg at around eighteen weeks of age and then lay an egg almost daily thereafter. In their first year, high-producing, well-fed backyard chickens will produce up to 250 eggs. After that, egg counts will naturally decrease each year, until the flock has to be replaced with younger layers.

farm-fresh eggs anyone?

After our flock started laying, we had a great little egg business going—$3 per dozen. Everyone in my office loved our eggs. Suddenly my move to the valley didn't appear so crazy to them after all. Mike took eggs to his office too, and Dianne was popular among the other moms at the boys' school. The second fridge in the carport that came with the house was perfect for storing our stash of eggs.

We discovered fairly soon, however, that there is a downside to farm-fresh eggs. Well—not to the eggs themselves. To the chickens. They are exceedingly messy. Every three weeks or so, it was time to clean the chicken coop. With all hands on deck, including the boys, we shovelled the now-yucky cedar shavings into wheelbarrows and pushed them out to the poo pile at the back of the barn. Yes, there really was a pile of poo. Probably not mentioned in the "Realtor's Guide to Country Living" pamphlet is the unsightly pile of manure behind the barn that grows on a daily basis. When we were new farm owners, just learning some of the finer points of agrarian life, I was horrified to discover that behind every barn on our street was a pile of manure, fondly referred to by all our neighbours as the "poo pile." And even worse, it gets added to every day as the stalls are cleaned out. Not being the person responsible for the barn chores, I managed to mostly ignore the ever-growing pile. But I was still relieved to discover that once a year the deposits to the poo pile are either offered to keen gardeners to ensure good crops or flowers or spread to fertilize the hayfield. Ah, so *that* was the smell we used to notice when we visited the valley in the spring! Manure has its uses, and thus the pile never reaches the roof of the barn and topples over. *Phew.*

To reward a job well done on chicken coop day, we'd all enjoy cinnamon buns and coffee (or milk) back at the house. Bill managed to avoid this stinky chore by assigning himself the task of making the coffee and setting out the cinnamon buns. Maybe he was the smart one, eh?

* * *

By the end of September, the construction crew was well ensconced, remodelling the ensuite and main bathrooms and the kitchen. We were helped greatly by a talented local interior designer who, besides modernizing the kitchen and bathrooms, drew up plans to accommodate a large soaker tub, a hankering from my infatuation with the other house we did not buy. She also introduced us to a terrific contractor who not only came with good ideas but also had the ability to stay within budget. Quite a few times during the reconstruction, I fell into the "Well, while you're at it…" trap. He would diplomatically point out the extra work, time, and cost my add-on idea would create, which most often squelched my enthusiasm. Having the reno guys in the house seemed to give Bill a daily focus. He joined them on their lunch breaks and enjoyed chatting to them. I did notice though that he was not able to pass along information to them or to make any decisions. If he and I had discussed an idea or wanted to talk to the contractor about options for flooring or bathroom fixtures, for example, Bill would ask him to call me at the office.

On weekends, Bill and I shopped nearby for locally grown organic vegetables and fresh homemade baking. In good weather, we could visit a farmers' market set up in the parking lot at the local church, with stalls and vendors selling their farm-grown produce. Also close by was a year-round "farm market" grocery store that sold only organic, fresh, locally grown produce. We barbecued delicious dinners, including fabulous lamb that had been raised just around the corner.

Love my great new wheels

Weather permitting, we borrowed Mike's ride-on mower and cut the lawn, which sounds like work but was great fun. I was surprised at Bill though. He wasn't into driving the mower. Yet he had always loved cars and driving. When we met, he owned a classic Volkswagen Beetle that he thought was wonderful, even though the floorboards were a tad leaky on the passenger side—a shortcoming I discovered the hard way on our first date. After that I insisted we take my car in wet weather. At that time, he had just sold a classic 1968 Buick Skylark convertible. It was baby blue and looked really hot in the picture Bill showed me. I'm sorry I never had a chance to ride in it. Over the course of our marriage, he had bought and sold a few vehicles, some to serve as replacement taxis should one of his cabs be off the road for repairs or maintenance, and some simply because he liked them. His current pride and joy was a white 1985 Chrysler LeBaron convertible with Mark Cross leather upholstery that he parked in front of the house for all to admire.

Given Bill's affinity for vehicles, I thought he would love driving the ride-on mower around the property. I imagined him, beer in the cup holder, sun hat covering his curls, zooming up and down the front and back lawns. Well, I couldn't have been more wrong. He got on the mower once, rode it for about five minutes, and then got off. That was okay because I loved riding it. But I was still surprised he didn't. A year or so later, I hired a gardener to come every couple of weeks. His heavy-duty mower could handle wet grass whereas ours could not, which left our yard looking pretty seedy when the summer weather turned wet for days.

* * *

Fall that year was golden. From September through to the beginning of November, the weather was like a second summer—warm to hot sunny days, coolish evenings, and, as I mentioned before, stunning sunsets. After dinner, we would go upstairs to tour the progress of the reno and then sit on the kitchen's outside deck, watching the sun go down as the horses peacefully grazed in our fields. *Our fields.* Those words gave me a warm sense of quiet or peace. Sadly, most of the Western world was not feeling quite as tranquil as we were. That fall is now known as the global financial crisis of 2008, the worst economic disaster since the Great Depression of 1929. It was a time of severe economic meltdown worldwide. We watched and read the news describing the subprime loans scandal, the mortgage foreclosures running rampant in the States as a result, and the cumulative effects of the mistrust within the banking community. (Note: this was pre-COVID-19, the financial ramifications of which will no doubt be analyzed by historians as having a much more devastating effect on the economy.) But for us, the only real estate repercussion would have been if we had decided to move back to the city after a year—a promise I had made to Bill if he didn't want to stay on the farm. Because real estate prices had bottomed out in the valley as well, we would not have been able to sell. We would have lost our shirts, along with so many others who suffered financially. Fortunately, that prospect never raised its ugly head and we continued to enjoy our new life.

Our first Thanksgiving on the farm was certainly a different experience. Traditionally we had hosted the family in our Vancouver condo. Dianne and Mike, subsequently joined by the boys, would drive in for a full-on roast turkey dinner. We would gather around my fancy dining-room table, set with the special-occasion silver, china, and crystal. Until she passed away in 2004, my mom would be at that table too, along with my stepdad George, who unfortunately had died of cancer in 2000. This year was the exact opposite. The commute was shorter for the kids, for one thing—a mere five-minute walk down the street. And instead of a formal tablecloth and the best wine glasses, our casual basement table was set with kitchen cutlery and everyday dishes. The food was still wonderful though. We feasted on a succulent turkey rotisseried by Mike, the family's official barbecue chef, accompanied by fresh organic veggies purchased locally. The plan was to start our own vegetable garden the following spring. We all said how thankful we felt to be together and living so close.

When cool evenings became downright chilly, and bright sunny days turned overcast and rainy, it was time to start winterizing the property, especially the barn and its activities. In the summer, the horses had been left out day and night, but come the fall they were brought in at night. After I was shown what to do, my favourite thing just before dark was to head across the backyard to the barn, open the big side door, and call to Sassy and Cassidy. They came running because they knew there would be yummy grain as well as a mound of fresh hay in their feeders, courtesy of Dianne. I was happy to take the credit for these goodies, should their horsey thinking tend in that direction. If for any reason the horses decided not to rush in, all I had to do was put some grain in a bucket and shake it. The stampede was on. As for the chickens, they came in at night all year round. I was supposed to shoo them into the coop, but as soon as it got dark, they all went in by themselves. Clever birds.

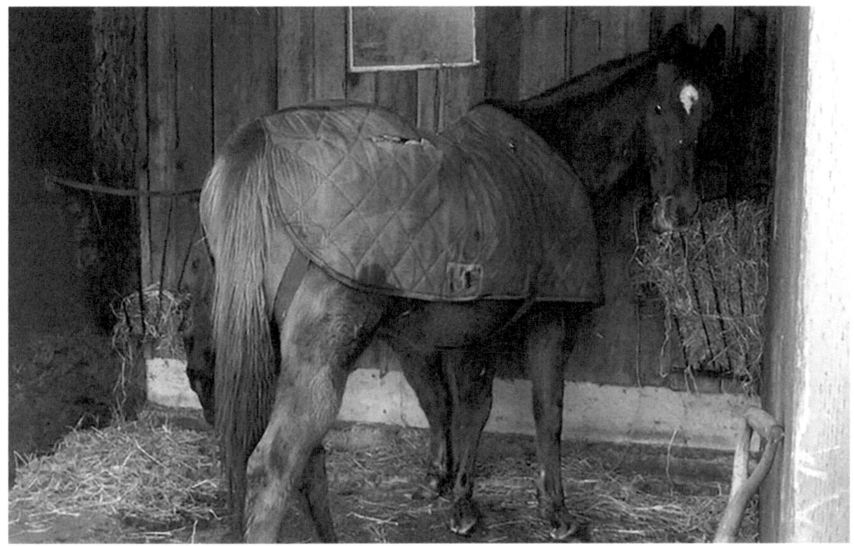

"Good job with the blanket"

Come the really cold weather, I also learned how to put the blanket on Sassy. Cassidy's coat was heavy enough that he didn't need a blanket, but sleek Sassy did. The first time I crawled between her back legs to fasten the blanket under her belly, I did feel some nerves. After all, in my precarious position, one excited hoof beat on Sassy's part could do some major harm, probably to one of my feet—or to my head, as I jumped up in surprise and pain. But at her age, Sassy was the epitome of calm. Her days of being skittish were pretty much over. At least that's what I chose to tell myself every time I fastened the blanket on her. When I told Bill after I put Sassy's blanket on the first time by myself, he had a fit. "You did *what?*" he croaked. After that I quit telling him the scary stuff.

Shortly after we got the chickens, we also purchased two llamas. This was Dianne's idea. There were coyotes living in the woods behind our property, and occasionally we'd see them running across the back field. For some reason coyotes don't go near llamas, but they sure love to attack chickens, as our neighbours across the road found out. Over the course of three nights, their entire flock was decimated. So two llamas installed in the field behind the chicken coop provided the perfect security system for our egg layers. Dianne bought the pair from a llama farm nearby. The owner offered to sell her one youngish female, named Willow, and give her for free Willow's much older male companion, named Mateo. The two llamas had been together for a few years, and the owner thought that Mateo would not do well after Willow left. As it turned out, Mateo lived happily for the next three or four years with Willow.

Willow waits for her treats too

Between them, the llamas not only fended off any chicken predators but were also a big hit with our visiting city friends, who loved to feed them horse treats. Willow was my favourite. Every morning when I let Sassy and Cassidy out after giving them their special treats, Willow would be peeking around the back of the barn, fluttering her eyelashes that were so long and curly they put any Hollywood femme fatale to shame, waiting for her share of the treats. How could I not love her? We all really liked Mateo too, but he was not as outgoing as Willow.

While I was learning how to tend to the horses and chickens, Mike and Dianne were starting to winterize the barn. The arrangement we had about the barn was that Dianne and Mike were in charge and responsible for its upkeep. They knew how to maintain a barn, while we did not. I was happy to be the novice helper; my job was to do what they taught me. When it came to barn activities, Bill was pleased to cheer us on from the house, making coffee for the "farmhands." He was not keen on hanging around one-ton animals with minds of their own.

Since this was the first year we'd been involved with this particular structure, Mike didn't know how our barn would fare during the cold weather. We hung rolls of heavy plastic on the inside walls of the chicken coop to keep the drafts to a minimum. After that, Mike installed heat lamps in the coop that stayed on day and night after the outside temperatures dropped down to freezing. He and Dianne checked the barn's plumbing and showed me how to turn off the water, should the pipes start to freeze. I wasn't exactly sure how I would know the pipes had started to freeze, but when (if?) I figured that part out, I knew I was ready. Mike also brought over his long ladder to investigate the barn's roof, which in his opinion looked solid. With all of that done, and winter just around the corner, how the barn would fare became a wait-and-see game.

* * *

Meanwhile Bill and I were still living in the basement suite, hoping we could move upstairs soon. Over a two-week period in November, all the new bathroom fixtures we had purchased arrived and were sitting in the carport, waiting to be installed. We enjoyed getting to know our neighbours as their curiosity prodded them to pop by to see what we were doing. Ours was the only soaker tub on the block with its own parking spot! When the snow started to fly, the contractors moved the impromptu bathroom inside.

For those of us living in the southwest corner of British Columbia, the winter of 2008 was the year Christmas was all but cancelled due to bad weather. The snowstorms and ice storms that hit the region wreaked havoc, causing power outages and traffic paralysis. Businesses were forced to close, residents were snowed in, and festive celebrations all but disappeared. We heard from many friends who could not get to their families' homes or whose guests could not get to theirs. Our own friends from Vancouver who we had invited to share our first Christmas dinner on the farm stayed home and ate cold sandwiches, since they had been unable to get to a grocery store in days.

In spite of all this, and with all due regret for everyone who was so inconvenienced for the entire months of November through February, I have to say that we loved the winter weather. And Christmas that year was our best ever. Traditionally, in contrast to Thanksgiving, Bill and I had been the long-distance drivers on Christmas morning. After Mike and Dianne had their kids, they quit making the trek into Vancouver and instead invited us to their place—a much more convenient arrangement with babies and toddlers in the house. So for the past seven years we had packed up the gifts and driven out to Abbotsford at the crack of dawn on December 25th, adhering to the strict instructions to arrive by 8:00 a.m. at the latest. You can't keep a pair of eager boys down much later than that on Christmas morning.

This year was so much better. Bill and I casually got up around 7:30 instead of the usual 6:00, picked up our bags of goodies, and strolled down the street. Total travel time: five minutes. En route we were enthralled by the absolute splendour and peacefulness of our entire neighbourhood. As a result of the many recent snowstorms, there were no car tracks. The road was ankle deep in fresh powder, and we were the only people out. The trees were bowing to us as we quietly passed by, their branches weighed down by the generous blanket of snow, and ice crystals sparkled everywhere in the just-rising sun, like some kind of fairyland. The quiet was overwhelming, the only sounds being the crunching of our feet in the snow. We held hands as we walked, saying nothing—just feeling at one with nature's breathtaking beauty.

Minutes later Mother Nature's aura became an instant memory as we were thrust into Dianne and Mike's Christmas morning mayhem: squealing kids, great presents, delicious eggs benedict brunch, a roaring fireplace, and an eggnog or two, since we had no driving to do. The lead-up to Christmas had been magical as well. I had taken three weeks off work, thinking the renovations to the house would be done and we could casually move upstairs and settle in. Alas, another batch of excited optimism down the drain. So there I was with nothing but time on my hands and a backyard full of snow. *Hmm. What to do?* Bring on the boys.

Fun in the snow

The three of us made snowmen, perfected our snow angels, baked Santa cookies, and drank gallons of hot chocolate, mine occasionally fortified with something a bit more substantial than just cocoa. Thanks to Dianne and Mike's efficient four-wheel-drive vehicle, we had no shortage of groceries and could still make shopping expeditions to the mall.

Bill and I had also borrowed Mike's ladder to string up our first-ever outdoor Christmas lights. City-slicker apartment dwellers do not do this sort of thing as a rule. Instead they wrap strings of mini lights around their balcony railings and spend December admiring their handiwork. Now we had photos of us taking turns up the ladder, bundled up so much against the cold that it was a miracle we could wiggle our fingers enough to screw in the hooks and attach the lights. Bring on the adult hot chocolate.

We shovelled snow too

As the freezing wind continued week after week, my *Little House on the Prairie* skills increased and improved exponentially. I learned how to carry water in buckets from the house to the barn through the knee-deep snow in the backyard because the pipes there were frozen (but the water had been turned off—yay me). I became an expert at how to scrape ice off the horse poop in the stalls to help Dianne shovel it into the wheelbarrow. So much for "I don't do stalls." And I never went out to the barn without a heavy-duty hammer that I used to break up the ice that had formed in the water troughs. I actually found smashing through five or six inches of ice to be useful therapy—especially after a frustrating day at the office.

The next year we sprung for a special coil heater that sits in the bottom of the trough, preventing the water from freezing. Thanks to Cassidy's thick coat and Sassy's warm blanket, the horses thought frolicking in the snow was a good time. The chickens were not quite so enthusiastic. They would peek out the door to their yard and then scramble back to their roosts. Whoever said chickens are dumb was wrong.

For Christmas, I was given ski gloves and a full-length down coat with a hood that came in very handy in that freeze-up. And on really cold days, I augmented my ensemble with a balaclava that covered my whole face. I used to think only bank robbers wore balaclavas. Who knew that for farmers, the Co-op displayed them for sale right out in the open? I learned a lot that first winter—survival skills that no lifelong condo dweller would even think of.

Love my balaclava

But it was gorgeous too

I don't usually get excited about New Year's Eve anymore. When I was in my twenties and maybe my thirties, I did all the traditional stuff: went to the crazy parties with the hats and horns, and made resolutions, both wise and ridiculous (like losing that perennial ten pounds). But I've never really been a devotee of the fact that the next day has a new date. Every January 1st, I'd look outside and see the same things I saw the morning before. Not that there was anything wrong with what I saw—it had just never been *new*. Same job, same car, same house, same ten pounds. Together, Bill and I were never big party hounds at New Year's either. We preferred bringing in a new year with a small group of special friends. Sometimes we hosted a dinner party, the kind where you sit around the dining-room table for hours just enjoying the company of people that you're really glad to have in your life. Other times we went out to dinner with just one couple.

Yet despite scorning all the hoopla around a new year, I am at heart an incurable romantic. So as our first New Year's Eve on the farm approached, I knew exactly what I wanted to do. To accomplish it, I had to enlist the help of a couple of strong guys and the contractor in charge of the reno, who, by mid-December, I had started to think of as a permanent fixture in the house. He had thought he would be out by Christmas, but a series of delays had made the project's finish date a moving target. At least he always sounded sorry when he had to say, "Not yet." And when I made my proposal to him, he was happily on side (probably motivated by guilt).

Bill and I were big fans of bathtubs. When he had acting gigs, he used to sit in the tub learning his lines. I guess he figured that by the time the water cooled off, he would have his part down cold, if you'll pardon the pun. When we paired up, we used to solve the world's problems while sitting together up to our necks in warm sudsy water. Trouble was, we were both six-footers, give or take an inch or two that Bill pretended he had but really didn't. With four long legs in a standard-size tub, often the only problem we would solve would be whose turn it was to hang a leg out over the floor. Thus the first fixture we bought in advance of the renovations was a large soaker tub, which the contractor and interior designer were challenged to fit into the master bedroom's old ensuite.

My special request was to be moved upstairs into the bedroom and the ensuite by dinnertime on December 31st. And the contractor made it happen. The guys downed tools in the kitchen and main bathroom to complete all the construction and decorating in the "tub room," as they called it. Then they hauled our five-piece bedroom suite up the stairs from the basement. New Year's Eve day saw me busily making up the bed, hanging pictures, and digging through boxes to find candles, the boom box, and appropriate CDs. Next I made a quick trip to the stores for champagne and appies, and then my plan was set.

After finishing a scrumptious rack of lamb dinner in the downstairs kitchen, Bill and I moved upstairs, filled the tub, and adjusted the lights. Then we lit the candles, put on the music, popped the cork, and settled into our wonderful soaker tub, no legs hanging over. A memorable first New Year's celebration in our new country life.

CHAPTER 6

Family affairs

JUST BEFORE OUR FIRST CHRISTMAS on the farm, we met Dr. David Chapman, the GP who would become our family physician and an integral partner in Bill's ongoing care. Before we moved to the valley, Dianne had offered to ask her doctor whether he was taking new patients. This was the first time I knew that doctors interviewed new patients to see if there was a fit. Were they looking for someone who wasn't too sick? Or someone who *was* quite sick? I never asked, and after the first five minutes in Dr. Chapman's office, I didn't care. He was a perfect fit for *us*. We liked his easygoing manner, his professionalism coupled with an obvious sense of caring, and his sense of humour. Apparently he liked us too, because as we shook his hand on the way out, we felt we were "in." And what a blessing that turned out to be.

Dr. Chapman was interested in the behavioural changes Bill had been undergoing in the past few years and what, if any, his medical treatment had been. When I described the anxiety disorder that had been diagnosed and Bill's subsequent depression, Dr. Chapman invited Bill to participate in a new program he was involved in that sought to help patients identify triggers for their bouts of depression. Called the BounceBack program, administered by the Canadian Mental Health Association and funded by the Provincial Health Services Authority, it featured a CD-ROM that contained insights into some of the causes of depression and outlined possible ways to relieve the anxiety. Key to the plan was the need to write out what made you feel down or upset or depressed. Next step was to implement the coping skills that had been described in the CD.

I thought this free program was a great idea and Bill was willing to try it. As it turned out, though, we never got around to implementing any coping skills, because Bill was not able to write anything down. He just stared at the blank paper, not understanding what he was supposed to say. It was like the concept of jotting down what had bothered him that day was beyond him. When I offered to help or prompted him, he got upset, and at one point I jokingly suggested that what depressed him was having to write down what depressed him. My attempt at humour missed the mark completely and he just looked at me. Then I tried asking him to *tell* me if there was anything that was upsetting him either at the moment or from earlier in the day. My thought was that being such a verbal person, he would be able to talk about his feelings. But he still just sat at the kitchen table looking at the paper. I wanted to hug him. Or give him a shake. Or cry. Or all three. I was absolutely mystified. And getting quite upset myself. *What was happening?*

When we reported this incident to Dr. Chapman, he wondered if Bill's confusion about the writing exercise might be the beginnings of Alzheimer's disease. He set up two tests used by health care professionals to assess patients' mental status. The MMSE (Mini–Mental State Examination) and the MoCA (Montreal Cognitive Assessment) tests each consist of a number of questions, the answers to which indicate a person's level of cognitive ability. Bill's results revealed a problem in this area. Dr. Chapman then prescribed Donepezil, also known as Aricept, a drug used to treat confusion (dementia) related to Alzheimer's disease. It does not cure Alzheimer's disease but has been known to improve memory, awareness, and a person's ability to function. Dr. Chapman said this was early stages and that the meds should help with Bill's confusion. At that point I hadn't noticed much in the way of memory loss for Bill, but I was definitely seeing signs of confusion.

Driving home from that appointment, I didn't know what to think. I didn't know what Bill thought either, or if he had even understood what the doctor had diagnosed. I hated to ask him. *What if he didn't understand? What if he did? And if he did understand that he had developed dementia, what would I say?* So I said nothing. I've read since then that it's important to be open with people living with Alzheimer's, especially in the beginning: to ask them what they understand and how they feel about it. Also to work on developing some coping skills—list-making, and so on. I wish I hadn't chosen to "sweep under the rug" this difficult topic. I didn't know much about Alzheimer's disease back then, even though it had started to get a fair bit of play in the media, and I didn't know what to do. I *had* heard that people with Alzheimer's needed to be mentally stimulated to slow down the progress of the disease. However, rather than call the Alzheimer Society of B.C. at this time to get some proper information, I stumbled along as best I could.

My plan was to try to keep Bill interested in daily activities and keep him busy. So far he wasn't a "roamer," so on the days that I went in to the office, I felt confident leaving him alone in the house. After working his way through the "honey do" list I left him, and if it wasn't a Co-op shopping day with Dianne, he often headed out for lunch on his own. Still driving, he would pop up to the local McDonald's at noon. Sometimes he would head into Vancouver for lunch with friends. This became worrisome after he got lost one time driving home from a friend's place in Surrey, a city located halfway between Abbotsford and Vancouver. He took the wrong on-ramp to the highway but didn't realize he was going in the wrong direction until he was halfway across the Port Mann Bridge, heading west instead of east.

On weekends we often entertained, since our friends were still keen to see how the "urban farmers" were faring. And Bill, a very social person at heart and an inveterate actor, perked right up when he had an "audience." He loved presenting friends with a dozen farm-fresh eggs that he had collected himself or pointing out how peaceful the horses looked grazing in the field. The next couple of years slid by without much change in his condition. Dr. Chapman monitored the progress of his symptoms and occasionally altered the dosage of his medication.

The day Dr. Chapman advised us of Bill's condition, he also asked us if we had our affairs in order. Did we have wills? Had we organized powers of attorney, and so on? We did have wills, but that was all. The doctor recommended we attend to the rest immediately, while Bill was still well enough to understand what he was signing. With Bill's dementia diagnosis and the fifteen-year age spread between us, it was suddenly apparent that we needed much more than just wills. I knew when I married a man a decade and a half older than I was that he would probably die before I did. But I hadn't expected the end of his life to come like this.

When I was growing up, my dad, who was also quite a lot older than my mom, had a heart condition that ultimately caused his death, leaving my mom and me on our own. Because of that, when I married Bill, my thoughts were "preprogrammed" that when he got old, he would have a heart attack and die and I would be a youngish widow. But he was too healthy to have heart trouble. His weight was just right; he was not on any meds for blood pressure or cholesterol or anything else. So until Alzheimer's disease came along, since he was physically fit, I had thought we were good for another ten years. It didn't matter that he was in his late seventies. Seventy had become the new sixty. But now I was being told to set up a regular power of attorney to handle his affairs and a representation agreement, which would enable me to make financial and health-related decisions for Bill while he was still alive.

Before seeking legal counsel, I sat down with Dianne. Bill had no other children and no siblings, so Dianne and her family would become the ultimate beneficiaries of our estates. As immediate next of kin, she was the logical one we would give decision-making power to, should something happen to both of us. Fortunately, she has a good business head on her and is responsible and honest. I invited her to lunch, our long-time favourite way to share information—good and not so good—and explained that the time had come to set up official and legal caregiving plans for Bill. She totally understood the situation and said she would be glad to join us at the lawyer's. We both realized Bill's condition would only get worse. What we didn't know was how fast his illness would progress.

The meeting at the lawyer's office was extremely enlightening vis-à-vis the responsibilities and restrictions of decision-making for a third party, both before and after death. The meeting also provided me with a great sense of "having my act together." We reviewed our wills, updated some of the clauses, and then turned our attention to our needs while we were still alive. The lawyer drew up a power of attorney document and representation agreement for Bill, which gave me the decision-making authority for financial and legal decisions as well as personal care and health care decisions. As Bill's wife, I could take over his affairs as required and increasingly did so during the progression of his disease.

At that time, Bill's ability to understand various situations came and went. Sometimes he seemed perfectly comprehending; sometimes he looked a little lost. The gamble or hope when we went to see the lawyer was that he would be having a "good day." I knew that the lawyer wouldn't let Bill sign any documents if he thought Bill didn't understand what he was signing. Fortunately, he was fine during the meeting, and while he didn't talk much, he also didn't say anything nonsensical. Through all this I was feeling bad. Talking about Bill as if he weren't in the room was sad, and discussing long-term options for his life as if we were deciding where to go for dinner felt awful.

Because of Bill's condition, I wanted to give Dianne my own power of attorney in case I should become disabled or incompetent in the future. Without actually saying it, though, I fleetingly wondered how this really worked—and whether she could start making decisions for me before I needed or wanted her to. Obviously, I had spent too many evenings watching movies about dysfunctional families. After I asked, the lawyer clarified what the parameters were for Dianne. She could not start calling my bank when she felt like it, just because she had my power of attorney. When she deemed it necessary to invoke her "power," she would need to receive written confirmation from my doctor that I was not able to handle my own affairs. Yay, Dr. Chapman. Then she would have to take that letter to the lawyer, who only then would give her the certified documentation.

The support we received from Dr. Chapman, coupled with the information and services provided by our lawyer, gave me confidence that our family affairs were now properly in order. It also put my mind at ease to know that everyone in the family was completely in the loop.

CHAPTER 7

Poodle people

AT FIRST, I HAD HOPED our relatively small reno would be completed by Thanksgiving. We were only ripping out two bathrooms and a kitchen—how much time should that take? Next hoped-for end date was November. Then definitely by Christmas. Unfortunately, the bad weather slowed everything down. Plus there were delays in the arrival of parts and fixtures as well as those caused by the occasional add-ons. By New Year's Eve, as I said, we were finally upstairs in the master bedroom and ensuite, with a promise to have all the rest completely done—painted and livable—by Valentine's Day. Finally, on February 2, 2009, Groundhog Day, we stood in our carport waving a fond farewell to the crew who had become such a big part of our life for the past five months. Their work was super and the house looked great—new modern bathrooms, a designer kitchen with more cupboards and drawers than I had ever had, plus an efficient and attractive island for prep work. In the bedroom, my favourite add-on was the new walk-in closet. We both loved the house, felt very settled once we were finally living upstairs, and we looked forward to finding a tenant for the basement suite we had just vacated.

> **FOR RENT**—Bright above-ground one-bedroom basement suite with all the mod cons, including a stacked washer dryer. Located on acreage in Aldergrove, the suite features a private entrance and parking for one vehicle. Monthly rent is reasonable and the landlords are terrific.

We rented to a young, newly married couple who were thrilled to get a place on acreage and turned out to be wonderful tenants for the next five years. Tim and Jess were quiet, paid their rent on time, and Tim helped around the place. The first winter they were there, I set up what I thought was a brilliant arrangement. For a reduction in rent from November to the end of February, Tim would shovel the driveway every time it snowed. If it didn't snow, lucky Tim - he still got the rent reduction. If it did snow, lucky me: I didn't have to worry about shovelling. We had an excellent relationship with Tim and Jess, friendly but maintaining a good sense of privacy. We were not in each other's pockets, and the arrangement worked well.

The initial rules I had created did not permit pets, but after a while, Tim and Jess asked if they could get a puppy. Considering that Bill and I were thinking of getting a dog ourselves, I could hardly say no, except that the backyard was not adequately fenced for a dog. But it soon was. By the time Tim and Jess had selected their new dog and ours was on the way, Mike and Tim had spent a weekend fencing in our large backyard. My participation in the fence project included cheering on the volunteer workers, bringing more beer, and paying the bill for the materials. Yikes! Who knew that the price for a 16-foot gate ranged from $150 to $300? Needless to say, I sprang for the $150 model. Then there was the mesh fencing to go along the side of the yard, stapled onto the wooden fence posts between our property and our neighbour to the west. The east side of the yard was already well fenced with cedar panels that separated the people from the horses. All told, we created a regular Fort Knox for dogs out back. This meant that Louie, our newly acquired standard poodle puppy, and Bentley, the tenants' cute puggle, could play out there unsupervised.

When we moved out to the farm, we had not planned to get a dog. And certainly not a poodle. When I think of farm dogs, I think of something more robust looking, like a golden retriever or German shepherd. But the idea of having a poodle just sort of snuck up on us. One weekend Dianne had been dog-sitting a well-trained and stately black standard poodle called Jack who won my heart. Poodles are very smart, everyone said, and they also don't shed—a great feature for those of us who are not in love with our vacuum cleaners. Plus they don't drool (hooray) and they're very dignified looking—definitely my kind of dog. Dignified worked for Bill too.

Our first farm poodle, Louie, was an apricot-coloured standard male. We got him as a pup and he was adorable. Unfortunately, after only three weeks with us Louie met with a tragic accident and died. Most people don't get another dog quickly after their pet dies, but in the few weeks we had had Louie, we'd discovered we really loved being doggy parents. Enter Cleo. She too was an apricot-coloured standard. She was born the end of April and came to live with us at the end of June 2009, almost a year into our amazing farm adventure. Cleo's colouring was different from Louie's, and she was definitely her own dog, with a friendly disposition and, like me, had an enthusiastic love of shoes. In addition, she was even smarter than the books said. In only one day she trained *us* to put away our clothes and shoes in the closet the second we took them off—and shut the closet door. Mounds of laundry? Done and hung up pronto, lest Cleo decide to help by scattering our unmentionables all over the house.

Bill and I had both come from cat families and didn't know much about owning a dog. The great thing about cats is you don't have to take them out. They take themselves out—to do their business or just play with unsuspecting mice that come within their line of vision. Or, if they're indoor cats, they have a cat box in the corner, which is even more convenient. But dogs need to be walked. Fenced yard notwithstanding, they need exercise, rain or shine.

I used to have a personalized licence plate that read "Wise 1." This was a joke that my colleagues in the office dreamed up when I worked at BC Women's Hospital. We were having a conversation about how some cultures revere and respect middle-aged women for their wisdom and experience. Since I was in my fifties at the time, and the oldest one in the department, the others decided I was their resident crone. Not the old folklore definition of a crone, an old woman who might be disagreeable, malicious, or sinister. No, I was the feminist or spiritual definition of a crone, transitioning into an era of wisdom, freedom, and personal power. So they called me the "Wise One," a title I accepted with much dignity and humility (tongue in cheek). Onto my licence plate it went, and when friends laughed, I told them it was my tribute to midlife. I had recently removed it from my vehicle though. It was not that I didn't feel wise anymore; I was just tired of the plate And I always suspected that if I did something stupid when I was driving, the driver behind me would think, "Wise 1 my ass!"

However, thanks to Cleo, I felt I had earned the title again. As the summer of 2009 was nearing an end and all the winterizing was taking place around the farm, I was busily winterizing Cleo. The beauty of having a deck off our downstairs family room was that it was right under the kitchen deck and protected from the elements (i.e., the rain). Step one in my wise plan was to teach Cleo to chase the ball and bring it back: a no-brainer for Cleo; she was a natural. Next we played ball with me throwing from my position under cover on the downstairs deck. Back came the ball from across the yard every time. Cleo was loving this. In my head, all was going to plan. We were set for winter.

At 7:00 a.m., the first morning with pouring rain, Cleo and I went down to the family room and out the sliding door to the deck, me with ball in hand. I could hardly contain myself, I felt so clever. I threw the ball. Out she dashed (presumably to retrieve the ball, but probably also thinking about her first morning call of nature). Back she came a second later, looking at me like I was crazy. What's going on out there? How can I go pee? *Hmm… I wasn't ready for that. I thought dogs loved being wet.* With a bit of cajoling and some enthusiastic "off you go" gestures on my part, desperation eventually won out and Cleo stepped gingerly onto the grass to do her thing. Soon she discovered the wonders of puddles, raindrops landing in her upturned mouth, and the amazing waterfall coming from the eaves (on the list to get fixed). It was so much fun watching her play in the rain—while also staying dry. Finally, all the cavorting around brought about her next required bodily function—is this getting too graphic?—and after that, Cleo and the Wise One went back inside.

But lest I forget, our bevy of family pets also included Sylvester and Tweetie, the two barn cats that came with the property. They had been part of a litter that was born six weeks before our possession date. When the vendors moved out, they took some of the kittens with them for their new farm and left these two females for us. Most farms have barn cats that live in the barn. Ours lived in the house. As I said, Bill and I came from cat people, and the kittens were so cute, we couldn't just leave them out in the barn. Also Matty and Kyle were crazy about the kittens. They each adopted one for themselves for when they came over to play. Matthew named his Sylvester, not knowing that was a boy's name (and I wasn't about to fill him in). Kyle named his Fluffy. But after I described for him the cartoons I grew up with about Sylvester and Tweety Bird, he agreed to change Fluffy' s name to Tweetie. A great improvement, I thought.

* * *

Christmas number two was different again from the previous year in that it came with a couple of new traditions—and a farm emergency. The first year we lived in Abbotsford, we often commuted Sunday mornings to Uhill, our regular church congregation at UBC, taking the boys with us. They were enrolled in the Sunday school there and participated in most of the children's activities. The trip was kind of a fun thing we did together and included lunch at McDonald's after church. Our second Christmas Eve on the farm, Matthew and Kyle, now seven and eight, came with us to Uhill's family service dressed in their pyjamas and housecoats so they could be shepherds in the kids' pageant and be simultaneously ready for bed when we later carried the two sleeping thespians into their home from the car.

Christmas Day and dinner were enjoyable once again, but memorable in a different way for Dianne. In addition to our small family group, Mike's sister had driven east from Vancouver and his mom, Carol, and her husband, Dan, were down for the holidays from their home in Summerland, in BC's Okanagan Valley. Early in the fall, Dianne had been hip-checked in her own barn by one of her horses, fallen, and suffered a seriously broken wrist. Surgery and six weeks in a cast, followed by six weeks of physio, definitely limited her farm and kitchen activities, including Christmas dinner. But never a group to miss a meal, we all pitched in, taking directions from our one-armed supervisor, and a perfect roast turkey made it to the table. Of course, being such a supportive mom, I also took over Dianne's barn chores for weeks, scooping the nightly droppings into the wheelbarrow every day and running them up the slippery hill of the poo pile. Yes, the poo pile raises its pungent head in my life again. Only this time it's me climbing the slippery mound with the wheelbarrow. This is progress?

Boxing Day 2009 brought its own surprises. The previous year we had been busy dealing with snow, ice, and frozen pipes. Year two, it was rain, more rain, and burst pipes. The morning of December 26, still smiling from the fantastic time we had all had the day before, I went out to the barn as usual and found myself squishing through a mess of soft, wet, floating poop. A water pipe had burst—*not* from freezing—and flooded the stalls, so I had to slip and slide my way down the shed row to check how the horses had fared. They were fine. My first line of defence during any emergency: call Mike. He threw on his clothes and dashed over to make the pipe repairs, and then we spent the next three hours mopping out the barn. More trips to the poo pile. Given a choice between chipping ice off frozen poop, like the previous year, or slopping through flooded poop, I would pick ice.

* * *

After two years, aside from unforeseen emergencies, I had the handling of winter storms down to a science. Early in January, the weather forecast was calling for a major dump of snow overnight in the valley. We were on it. I simply referred to the comprehensive list I had created:

Buck's Fail-Safe Directions for Enjoying a Stress-Free Whiteout

1. Bring the horses in early.
2. Replenish the grain in each stall's feeder.
3. Bring the chickens in early. Oh, they're already in—smart chickens.
4. Check the water pails and chip off ice if necessary.
5. Call Tim downstairs to remind him where the snow shovels are.
6. Bring a bottle of red wine up from the wine rack downstairs.
7. Warm the wine in a small saucepan with mulled wine spices.
8. Prepare a few nibblies, such as cheese and crackers—nothing too fancy.
9. Fill the two-person soaker tub with hot bubbly water.
10. Light the candles in the bathroom.
11. Bring in two mugs of steaming mulled wine and the appies.
12. Climb into the tub with the hubby, lean back, and relax.
13. Wait for the snow!

The Morning After

1. Take two aspirins. Must have been the spices in the mulled wine.
2. Pull on barn boots, coat, balaclava, gloves, and scarf, and head out into the stillness of a winter wonderland.
3. Let the horses out. They go—silly horses.
4. Open the chickens' door to the yard. They don't go—clever birds.
5. Back in the house, listen to the traffic report. Smile a lot. Gotta love these farm snowstorms when you have nowhere to go.

CHAPTER 8

Downhill slide

EARLY IN 2010, BILL'S DEMENTIA symptoms began to worsen. It had been a year since his diagnosis. Initially he didn't seem much different from before we moved to the farm. Some days he was up and at' em with energy—looking for breakfast, wondering what we were doing later, or making plans to meet an ACTRA friend for lunch. Other days were downers for him, when he was lethargic and at times confused. For me, the stress was not knowing "which Bill" was going to appear next. Or which one would be there when I got home from work. It was really hard to stay calm and go along with each moment's situation. I started to keep a diary, thinking it would come in handy for the doctor—and for me. It worried me that because I was on edge much of the time, I might be overreacting to Bill's behaviour changes. Or, maybe not reacting enough. Should I give the doctor more information?

Tuesday, February 16

Bill was up in the night three times, thinking it was time to go out somewhere. He got completely dressed, then woke me up to say he was off. He thought I had taken a message on the phone from his agent. He thought the movies were calling. I told him his agent never calls in the middle of the night and he should wait til morning. Then I helped him back into his pyjamas and bed.

It's worrisome for me that I'm such a sound sleeper. What if he just heads out the door in the middle of the night and starts roaming around the neighbourhood?

This waking in the night has been happening quite frequently over the past couple of weeks. But usually only when he has an actual appointment to get to the following day. Today there was nothing on—we had no plans. It's really hard for me to stay patient and not let my frustration goad me into getting mad at him. Interrupted sleep doesn't help either. It's good to have a friend in the same boat. Irene and I are going through the same things with our husbands and we compare notes a lot. "How long did it take you before you lost your cool?" we ask each other. I really hate myself sometimes because when I get exasperated, I start talking to Bill in a voice that sounds like something from that *Mister Rogers* children's TV show. It sounds like I'm talking to a child. I feel terrible but can't seem to help myself. Irene and I encourage each other to not get mad at Bill and Ted. "Remember, it's not their fault," we say. "It's so sad."

Thursday, February 18

Bill slept through last night. He was still asleep when I went to work. I called around noon and he was up—nothing extraordinary about our conversation. Dianne and Mike and the boys came over for dinner tonight to watch the Winter Olympics. Partway through the evening Bill started a nonsense conversation, asking if he had received a phone call about the movie he was expecting to hear about. It sounded like he thought he had auditioned for a part and was hoping for a callback.

His speaking voice is unbelievably soft now and weak sounding. Dianne and Mike hadn't seen him doing this before. They were shocked and asked me how I stayed calm when it happened. Guess they know that patience isn't one of my biggest virtues. How *do* I stay calm? I don't know. Sometimes I think my "mother gene" kicks in and my mind thinks I'm talking to a child who's making no sense. Maybe *I*'m the one who's losing it.

Monday, February 22

Last Thursday night Bill had such a restless night that I had to move into the other bedroom. He was having dreams that caused him to punch out and throw himself around the bed. I was actually worried he would hit me.

Friday night he was fine.

Saturday, we took my car in to have the snow tires taken off, then went into Langley to run a couple of errands and he was fine.

Sunday was a good day. Bill did laundry. I met with Dianne to plan the veggie garden I want to plant this spring. Then we went with Di to dinner at the White Spot.

Last night, Bill had a good sleep.

* * *

On Fridays, my day off, we always went to a gym at a local sports centre where we joined a class of seniors who did gentle exercises three times a week. I had been told that exercise is good for the brain and thought it might do mine some good too. There were about thirty in the class, mostly women in their late seventies and beyond, with varying levels of ability. The instructor led the group from the front, and participants formed six or so rows of about five each in a large workout room. The exercises were medium-fast to slow moving, with everyone being encouraged to go at their own pace.

Like all exercise classes, this one started with a warmup, which comprised step and arm movements accompanied by loud music. I always situated us in the back row, away from most of the others. Bill didn't keep up well during the warmup, which could make him a bit of a distraction. He never did have a good sense of rhythm—his one big flaw (and he couldn't dance either, but nobody's perfect). During the rest of the program too, he didn't fully understand the exercise routines being demonstrated by the instructor. But by staying at the back of the room, I could help him and keep him out of everyone's way. He seemed to enjoy the outings and always offered the others a friendly smile or "hi."

This weekly activity was working quite well, I thought. But after we'd been attending for a few months, the instructor pulled me aside one day as everyone was filing out of the room. "I think this group isn't where you and Bill should be," she said. "You should switch to the class that runs just after ours. It's for people who need a slower pace." She added that Bill's inability to keep up was upsetting others. I was crushed that she would think Bill was a problem. It felt like we were being thrown out of the class for bad behaviour. And I was instantly angry that she would make this pronouncement in such a heartless way, and in front of others who were still in the gym. I had been so pleased with how much he enjoyed attending the class, and I enjoyed helping him with the moves. I felt insulted and also devastated for Bill, who didn't know what had happened.

Besides giving us some exercise, this was also a social outing. Every week after class, most of us stayed for coffee in the lounge just outside the gym—the women at one table and the half-dozen or so men banding together across the room. Bill always went with the men and, from where I was sitting, seemed to join in. Everyone knew he had dementia. It was very obvious. But everyone was really nice to him.

I was so stunned by what the instructor had said, I mumbled we'd give the other class a try. But we didn't. Instead I went directly to the manager's office to complain and demand our membership fees back. I was incensed. "For a fitness instructor with experience leading groups of people, particularly seniors, she obviously does not have a clue how to broach a sensitive subject with a class participant," I said. Then I added that friends I had made in the class said they had not heard any negative comments about Bill's presence. The manager agreed with me that the instructor's approach was totally uncalled for and unprofessional. He also agreed to refund our membership fees. I told him I had no intention of belonging to a health facility that treated its members so badly. Friends I told asked me if I was embarrassed for Bill about this. My instant response was, "No, I'm embarrassed for the gym and the instructor. What's wrong with them?"

* * *

By late winter, I started to notice that Bill's condition was worsening even more. Thursday nights, after being alone in the house for the four days in a row that I was at the office, his depression and anxiety were at an all-time high. He was spending most of his days in bed and often didn't eat—or he drove out for a Big Mac. It took him the whole three-day weekend that I was home to relax back into his regular, not-great but not-that-bad self. In light of Bill's illness, in June I made arrangements with my boss to cut back my workweek to three days from four. I would also work from home two of those days, thereby commuting to Burnaby only on Tuesdays.

Love working from home

The new setup was like living in seventh heaven. I set up my laptop on the downstairs covered deck and worked to my heart's content, looking up from the computer screen occasionally to watch the horses grazing or the chickens running around in their yard. I was getting lots of work done, keeping in touch with the office all day by email and phone, and also helping to reduce Bill's anxiety levels by being home. I was able to give him a proper lunch and make a short "honey do" list every day that kept him physically and mentally more active than when he was spending the days in bed. My Tuesdays in the office were enjoyable and productive times for me, and I suspect that Bill was probably happy to have me out of his hair for one day a week—bring on a Big Mac. With this new work schedule, I was happy, Bill was happy, and I thought my boss was happy. Well, two out of three ain't bad.

Come autumn, the leaves were almost all off the trees, the laptop was back inside, and I was given the word. I had to return to working in the office two days a week. My boss didn't like it that I was only in on Tuesdays and wanted me in on Fridays too. This was not good. The "summer of our great content" was over. The problem was, in spite of my presence all summer, Bill's condition had continued to slip and he was always anxious and unsure of what to do. When I asked him to, he went out to the barn to let the chickens out, but sometimes he couldn't remember why he was there or how to do it. He also got confused about what day it was, what time it was, and what we were doing that day. And he still sometimes got up and dressed in the middle of the night. He couldn't prepare food for himself, except for cereal, and a diet of fast-food hamburgers was out of the question. He could no longer be safely left alone all day in a large house with acreage all around it.

Ironically, my boss herself solved our dilemma. At first I was furious with her for insisting that I leave Bill alone two days a week. I phoned our financial advisor to talk about the possibilities of early retirement (he laughed). Then I called a lawyer to see if she could do this to me (she could). But it was my boss who told me it was time I contacted the local public health authority to discuss what services were available. She also said the Kidney Foundation had a long-term care disability plan that covered in-home care for spouses. In the long run, she really did us a favour by insisting I work in the office that extra day.

After I made a few calls, I was able to get an appointment with a delightful and helpful nurse from the Fraser Health Authority who was assigned as our case manager. She came to the house and explained how the system worked, saying it was good to have Bill registered. "As his health needs increase, I'll know what services he has already received and will be able to advise you on next steps," she said. First she put Bill on the waiting list to attend an adult day program offered at Maplewood House, a long-term care facility nearby, on one of the days I worked. "A couple of hours of home care are also available on the other day that you would be at work," she continued. In addition, I learned that primary caregivers—that would be me—are given four weeks' respite care a year. During that time

Bill would move into a care facility, so I could have a break. For Bill, the respite care facility would be the residents' wing of Maplewood House. Caregivers could take their four weeks in one-week periods throughout the year or all at once. The cost of the respite care was very reasonable, and in my case, was covered by my company's extended health benefits. My forced return to the office was what we needed to get organized for the next stage of our lives.

After some weeks, an opening came up for Bill at Maplewood on Fridays. The first day I dropped him off was an emotional roller coaster for me. I was happy, relieved, and broken-hearted all at once. But the action of getting Bill up, dressed, fed, and into the car by 9:00 a.m. came so naturally to me it was like total déjà vu.

> **Question:** What is the difference between a single mother with a child in daycare and a wife with a husband in daycare?
>
> **Answer:** Thirty-nine years.

It was early 1972 when I took two-year-old Dianne to daycare for the first time so I could go back to work. I dropped her off and with a big encouraging smile and a quick kiss, I waved goodbye as she was led into the playroom to meet the other kids. Back in the car, I burst into tears. Early in 2011, I repeated the process. This time with seventy-nine-year-old Bill. I took him to the adult day program and went in to meet the staff and see the place. After giving him a big encouraging smile and a quick kiss, I watched a very nice woman introduce him to the others who were also registered for the men's program, and usher him into the activity room. Back in the car, I burst into tears.

That was the dry run (*dry* run?) since I wasn't going in to the office that day. If adult daycare didn't work out for Bill, I would be making other arrangements. Quitting work and applying for welfare was my first (slightly irrational) thought. Thankfully, when I picked him up five hours later he was chipper and enthusiastic about the day he'd had. Bill was very social, so I knew in my heart that this program would be good for him, and 100 percent better than staying in the house all alone. But having a husband who was starting to behave like my young child had done was soul destroying. So was the fact that now the "child" was driving the parent to daycare. Since on office days I had to be out of the house by 7:30, and the daycare program ran from ten to three, Bill became part of Dianne's Friday routine. She would take the boys to school, then pick up Grampa and take him to daycare. Later she would pick up the boys after school, then pick up Grampa and take him home. I had waitlisted Bill for another day in the adult day program and was making arrangements for a couple of hours of home care too.

Soon I noticed that my years as a single mom paid off in many of the situations I was facing. It's almost scary how easy it was to drop back into the old routines, such as dressing, toileting, brushing teeth, and giving constant reminders and help with transitions. But when it came to home routines, I learned the difference between asking a child to set the table or do chores that are within their capability and asking someone with dementia to help. If the child puts the cutlery on the wrong side of the plates, you show them the right way. If your husband reverses the knives and forks, you just come along behind and switch them yourself—or don't. The difference is, you're teaching the child the correct way to do a task, and eventually they will learn. The person with dementia will never do it better. Today they are the best they will ever be. Tomorrow? Who knows?

One day when I was out walking with Cleo I bumped into Gerry, our next-door neighbour. He was driving his UTV up the street, with Buttons ensconced on the passenger seat enjoying his afternoon "walk." Gerry asked me if I knew that Bill was becoming a roamer. He told me that sometimes he or Rose would look out their front window and see Bill striding up the street towards Bradner, the main road at the end of our cul-de-sac. "Sometimes he comes right back, sometimes not," Gerry said. He further explained that when they saw him, one would say, "There goes Bill." And the other would say, "Let's wait five minutes, then I'll go get him." If they didn't see Bill pointing back towards home, either Rose or Gerry would get in their vehicle and head up the street looking for him. Usually they picked him up before he got to the end of our street.

Bradner Road was not too risky, but a mile to the north, it crossed the dangerously busy Fraser Highway. Across the four lanes of traffic was a gas station and convenience store that offered all sorts of goodies Bill liked: chocolate bars, cans of Coke, and bags of chips. Bill had developed a desire for junk food and this store was his mecca. One day Gerry and Rose didn't see Bill leave home, but fortunately Gerry was going out anyway, and just as he reached the highway, he saw Bill heading back down the hill, chomping on a Snickers bar, and he brought him home. It was right after Gerry filled me in that I got word there was space for Bill in daycare one more day a week. *What a relief.*

These were challenging times. My goal was to keep Bill as healthy as possible and living at home for as long as possible. I couldn't imagine how upsetting it would be for me and for him to have Bill living in some sort of long-term care home. My other goal was to get signed up for a support group for myself. I was getting pretty stressed out, and comparing notes with Irene, my girlfriend whose husband also had dementia, was not enough. But where would I tell Bill I was going? "Gotta go out for a while, honey. Tonight is my *learn to live with your demented husband group meeting.*" That sounded like a line Niles Crane would say on a *Frasier* rerun. (I warned you that humour, even the dark kind, was one of my coping strategies.) Anyway, more self-care and support was on my list of things to get figured out. Meanwhile, I just carried on carrying on.

* * *

September 7, 2011, Bill's eightieth, dawned hot and sunny, perfect for his usual Labour Day weekend celebration. Thanks to the lawn furniture we had and the tables and chairs I borrowed from the kids down the street, we were set for a great time in the backyard. I'd invited about two dozen friends to help Bill celebrate this milestone, and they all came, including a few of the nearby neighbours. Guests included two couples from the church, among them Alan Reynolds, the minister who had married us, and his wife, Brenda, and three of Bill's great pals from his CBC days—Bill Reiter, Norm Grohmann, and Bruce Macleod, our best man, who had skipped out of his high-school reunion early to dash out to the valley for Bill's big day. We had lots of laughs and excellent food thanks to Mike at the barbecue. It was super to see everybody, and Bill loved the fun and attention. With September 10 being grandson Kyle's birthday, we had our usual shared celebration, and both the birthday boys blew out the candles on the giant cake together.

Later that night, sitting on the back deck, glass of wine in hand, Bill and I talked about how wonderful it was that so many friends came out to see him. Unfortunately, I also remembered a short conversation I had had with the CBC trio. They were standing apart from the crowd, heads together, looking concerned. When I approached them to see what was up, one of them said, "Bill doesn't seem to quite know what's going on." The other two just nodded. There wasn't much I could say, except to also nod in agreement and mutter something brilliant like "I know." Truth is, I could barely say anything at all for the big lump in my throat. But I was also secretly glad that they had noticed Bill's behaviour. I knew at some point I would turn to them for their support, even if my need was unspoken at that moment. I didn't want to say the *d* word. I'm sure they didn't want to hear it either, but I know they knew. So far I'd kept Bill's diagnosis within the family. I didn't know whether they'd all see Bill again—or whether he would know them if they did meet up. But I was thankful for the great day we had had.

CHAPTER 9

More pâté, anyone?

STANDING IN THE KITCHEN AT 2:00 a.m. with a can of puppy formula in one hand and a tiny syringe in the other wasn't where one would expect to find any self-respecting grandmother, let alone me. But there I was, getting ready to hand-feed two ten-day-old poodle pups in the middle of the night. My nocturnal feeding adventure had started ten days before with the saga of Duchess, Dianne's standard poodle, the matriarch of her fledgling poodle breeding business. Duchess had had a litter of twelve pups. Sadly, three had died, but, from a breeder's perspective, a litter of nine is exceptionally viable.

On the day the pups were born, we all stood around and admired mother and babies. On day two, "mother" was not looking well. She threw up what looked like part of a toy and she wasn't eating. Duchess was rushed to the vet, where she received major surgery to remove a bowel obstruction that turned out to be the rest of the toy, and came home to resume her mothering duties. Unfortunately, two days later she was back at the vet. She had developed a uterine infection caused by her weakened state and the energy she expended caring for her pups. To treat this, she was put on a course of antibiotics that prevented her from nursing. When she came home that time, she was so agitated at being separated from her babies that Bill and I brought her over to our house for recuperation and to save her the angst of hearing her pups cry.

Duchess, with her curly black coat and stately long legs, was an elegant and dignified dog whose nature was so gentle, it was no wonder she wanted to continue caring for her babies. Cleo, the poodle we already had, kept her company during her convalescence. On Duchess's first trip to the vet, not knowing when Duchess would be back or if she would be able to nurse, Dianne got puppy formula from the pet store and invested in a number of tiny syringes. Mike, Bill, and I all lined up for the lessons. Here is what we were taught: Fill the syringe to the 10 ml line with formula. Weigh the pup on the kitchen scale. Hold the pup on its back in the palm of your hand. Insert the tip of the syringe into its mouth. Squeeze the syringe to expel one-tenth of the formula. Wait for a second or two till that bit goes down, then squeeze again. When the pup has ingested 10 ml, it's time to get it to pee. *What?* Animal mums massage their offspring to stimulate urination and defecation. So gently massage the pup's lower belly until it "produces." Then weigh it again. If the scale moves up a touch, the feeding has been a success. Finally, place each pup in the separate box that has been prepared with a heating pad and towels.

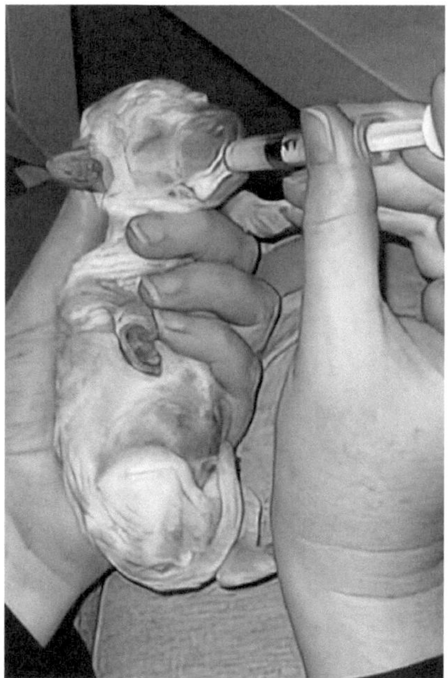

Trust me, little one. The syringe is your friend

This procedure sounds relatively simple, right? Here's what real life actually looked like. First, the pup wiggles so much on the scale, it falls off. Fortunately, the drop is only a couple of inches, so no damage is done. Next, holding the pup in the palm of your hand requires at least four other human hands to secure its flailing paws and wiggly head. Then there's the part where the pup already knows how to clamp its jaw shut. Three days old and we have nine natural fighters on our hands. However, if you wrap the pup up in yards of paper towel, this reduces the wiggling and helps keep the human dry. Squeeze 1 ml, wipe the spat-out formula off your trousers, readjust the paper towel, and squeeze again. After 15 minutes, the syringe is empty. How much formula went in and how much went on is questionable.

Pee-pee time made me laugh out loud. The male pups responded just like boy babies having their diapers changed. A steady stream of urine arched up in the air and landed on their tummy. This reminded me of the times I didn't duck fast enough when I was changing my grandsons.

When Duchess was at the vet's for surgery, we realized that hand-feeding nine wee puppies could turn into a three-week, 24/7 effort. We put our heads together for another solution. I'm proud to report that *I* came up with the brilliant idea that we should try to find a surrogate nursing mom. *Thank you… Thank you very much.* Enter Moxie, a golden retriever who belonged to one of Dianne's friends. Moxie's pups had just been weaned but she still had some milk. Mike was dispatched to get her. We all waited with bated breath to see whether this idea would work. After arriving at the poodle nursery, Moxie went into the whelping pen, lay down, and the pups headed right for her. Perfect. The next day, when Duchess came back from her first trip to the vet, we all said thanks to Moxie, rewarded her with a yummy-to-her bone, and moved her out to socialize with Duke, the pups' dad. Honest, Dianne didn't name these dogs Duke and Duchess—they came with those names.

After Duchess's second trip to the vet, when the antibiotics prevented her from continuing to nurse, Moxie, who was still at Mike and Dianne's, was reinstated and continued to feed the pups. But because it wasn't known if her milk was still rich enough for three-day-olds, supplementing had to continue. For the next few days, Mike and Dianne were back in the land of new parents with a tiny baby. They started to take on that look I had seen when each of the boys was just home from the hospital—red, sleep-deprived eyes with lids that can hardly stay up. They took turns feeding the pups every four hours, a job that took an hour each time because the wiggly critters just didn't get it that the syringe was their friend. Some of the pups were thriving; some were still quite small but hanging in there. In a follow-up call about Duchess, the vet told Dianne she was doing a fabulous job with the pups; he was amazed that she had saved them all. And after a couple of days, Moxie seemed to be producing enough milk that the larger, stronger pups did not need supplementing.

A week later, Duchess's meds were finished and out of her system, so the vet said to try putting her back with the pups. While most of the litter stayed with Moxie, the two smallest pups were brought over to our place to be with their mom. Duchess was really glad to see them and started caring for them right away. Now *I* was the sleep-deprived parent with the droopy eyelids, supplementing Duchess's milk supply at 2:00 a.m. And I was loving it. I was in a state of wonder—partly that a surrogate dog could step in and take over for the sick mom. Partly that the real mom was still so interested in her pups after all she'd been through. Partly because the pups were so darn cute. And mostly that my daughter loved animals so much, she had learned how to do all this stuff. These pups were the beginning of a highly successful breeding business that Dianne still runs. Duke and Duchess were the first doggy parents.

* * *

After Duchess's surgery and recovery, she stayed at our house. I had grown really fond of her, and she and Cleo played together well. But Bill and I soon discovered that life with two dogs is never dull. One day I took Cleo to the vet because she had a stomach infection of some sort, probably from eating mouse leftovers that Sylvester or Tweetie had proudly brought to the back door. The two of us were sent home with a mitt full of pills, a half-empty wallet, and the encouraging words that Cleo would stop upchucking right away. My first attempt to just pop open her mouth and toss a pill down her throat met with disaster. She had no interest in gobbling down the pill I was gently offering, and to the inexperienced, attempting to pry open a dog's mouth is a daunting task. Eventually, with a bit of risky brute force, I did get one into her, but I was starting to despair about doing this twice a day for the next week. Then I remembered the words of wisdom that John, our great friend from Gabriola, had shared once, after he tried to administer medicine to a cat—one of life's impossibilities. "Bury the pill in some pâté and the pet will lick it right up," he had said. *Great idea.*

There being an absolute lack of pâté in my fridge, I thought peanut butter would be just as good. At puppy training classes I had attended with Cleo, one of the "doggy dads" had encouraged his very tiny pup with peanut butter on the end of a wooden spoon, to save him the trouble of bending over every two minutes to give the treat. Following John's lead, I put a dollop of peanut butter, the crunchy kind to help hide the pills, on two spoons—one for each of the dogs. (I could not get away with giving Cleo something special and not giving something to Duchess.) And, being the clever dog psychologist that I am, and student of TV's "Dog Whisperer" Cesar Millan, I offered the peanut butter to Duchess first, knowing Cleo would want whatever Duchess was having. What I hadn't counted on was Duchess *no*t wanting the treat. And sure enough, she turned her back on the peanut butter. Walked right away. And right on cue, Cleo did too. So it was back to "Open wide. This will make you feel better." Then I dashed off to Safeway for one of those tubes of inexpensive but tasty pâté mixtures you can find in the deli section with the overpriced cheeses and gourmet olives.

Twelve hours later I got out the pills, the tube of pâté, and two spoons. This time I hit pay dirt. Within seconds the pâté and pill were down the hatch, and Duchess loved getting the bonus treat. Next day when I went to dispense the meds, all my spoons were in the dishwasher, so mindlessly I went to the other drawer and got out two small silver teaspoons. *You have to be kidding,* I thought as I realized what I was doing. *Now I'm feeding two dogs pâté from silver spoons! Give me a break.* But my method continued to work and the silver spoons were just the right size, so I kept using them. Every time I was standing at the counter where the medication was, I was joined by two expectant faces, tongues lolling and tails wagging. Needless to say, my popularity waned when the prescription was finished and the pâté treats came to a sudden end. But until then, what a posh life these two led.

A few weeks later, Dianne and I had a conversation about the dogs. She had added goldendoodles to her line of puppies that she was breeding and needed female poodles, already being the owner of golden retrievers. Since Duchess's surgery, Dianne had decided to miss a heat and not breed her again for a while, to make sure she had regained all her strength. Cleo was now coming into her second heat and could be bred. So it was decided that Cleo would move down the street to Dianne's, and I would keep Duchess. Then in a few months, when the time was right, Duchess would go to Dianne's for a "sleepover" and come back to my place till her puppies were due. This worked out well for me because having two dogs was getting to be a bit much, and I really liked Duchess. She was older and not as rambunctious in the house as Cleo, which made her easier to have around. I became official mom to a "duchess." Did that make me Lady Buck?

* * *

I loved Saturday mornings. The house was peaceful and quiet, the only sounds being the coffee pot gurgling its way to ready and the occasional peep from Sylvester, the barn cat–cum–house cat, stretching and rolling over on the couch. (Tweetie wasn't there. She preferred to live rough in the barn.) As I sat at the kitchen table, my view out the windows at the barn and fields was a study in peace and contentment. The horses serenely munched their breakfast of second-cut hay that I had tossed out to them that morning, and the chickens pecked for bugs in their special fenced yard.

Soon the morning peace would be broken. Bill would be up and rummaging around in the kitchen, getting coffee and cereal. The family would all be over—Mike and Dianne to do the barn chores, and the boys rushing in to tell me their latest news. One week, Matthew was all excited about a birthday party he had been invited to. Kyle was choked because he wasn't invited too, so his mom promised some other outing just for him instead. One Saturday Bill and I had to borrow Mike's pickup truck to buy two new panels of cedar fencing. The wind had blown down part of the fence that divided the side field from our backyard. Until we got that fixed, we couldn't put the horses out, or they'd wander into the backyard and be peeking through our back door in no time. While we were at the lumber yard, we purchased white paint for the front fence. Where is Tom Sawyer when you need him?

Despite the work and maintenance "surprises," I must say I was enjoying rural living, especially our egg business, which turned out to be a great little profit centre. We collected the money—all in coins—in coffee mugs in my kitchen cupboard and raided the stash when it was time to buy supplies for the chickens and cinnamon buns to reward the family after the monthly coop cleanup. And when the expenses were taken out, there was always money left. After a year of being farm-fresh egg entrepreneurs, we had netted over $300. Dianne's job, as the family accountant, was to count and roll the coins. My job was to help plan how to spend our earnings.

Our first major purchase was an above-ground swimming pool for the backyard, complete with a slide and water filtration system. Canadian Tire was having a sale that we couldn't resist. The pool was installed in our yard rather than the kids' yard, since we had more room, and it was the perfect place to cool off anytime. The boys loved coming over to our place for a swim that summer, and the adults found themselves languishing in the cool waters on many hot weekend days or evenings. The pool also turned out to be an excellent location to watch the Abbotsford International Airshow. In our first year with the pool, the prevailing winds sent all the main airshow entries over our house. It didn't get much better than watching the Canadian Forces Snowbirds perform their aeronautical acrobatics while sitting chest deep in cool water on a hot day, with a beer in your hand, of course. Occasionally we turned, cans raised in tribute, to offer a toast of thanks to the chickens, which—between flyovers—we could hear clucking in their yard just behind us.

An unfortunate fact for us city transplants to discover was that the first group of chickens we had brought home would not be our lifelong hens. The "girls" had reached an age where the number of eggs they were laying was so small they were not covering their costs, so they had to be replaced. Out came the wire cages again, and with Mike's help, we took the hens to the weekly farm auction in Langley. Some of the birds were bought by people who wanted only a few eggs a day for their immediate family. Others were purchased as meat for soups and stews—not for roasting, for they were too tough. I didn't like to think about that part of having chickens.

Back at Echo Hatchery, we bought fifty more young layers to add to our barn family. Besides learning where to find the water and food in their new home, new birds take a while to acclimatize to the daily routine. As I've said, usually when it got dark, the chickens all headed back into the coop by themselves. This made the bedtime routine on dark nights easy for me. I didn't have to do anything to settle them in except shut and lock their door. But these new hens took a while to figure out the routine. One morning, when I went out to open their door, I saw a chicken wandering around in the yard all alone, having spent the night outside probably wondering where her mates had gone. I took pity on her and thought I would catch her and put her back in the coop before the others came out, so she could eat and get some water.

As I was chasing her around the yard, being careful not to fall because the yard was slippery with chicken doo-doo, the Bible story about the good shepherd searching for the one lost sheep flashed into my mind. Not that I compared myself to the good shepherd, or that I compared a confused chicken to a wayward sheep, but I did wonder if the shepherd too was worried that he would slip and land in a pile of yuck. Then I wondered why I was bothering to chase this crazy bird around the yard at all. Why not let her stay put? She would eventually figure out the routine. But before I could argue too much with myself, I caught the errant hen and popped her through the door of the coop. According to the Bible, the shepherd celebrated that he had found his one lost sheep. I guess I was glad too.

* * *

Having lived in the rural part of Abbotsford for three years, I had pretty much made the transition from being a transplanted Vancouverite to being a true Abbotsfordian—and more than that, one who lived on a farm. No city-girl habits for me any more. I was into *au naturel*. I went to the store without mascara on and often didn't bother with lipstick. However, I did keep my standing appointment with the manicurist. Certain standards were unshakeable.

How times had changed. In my early days, how you looked—especially on the street—was of utmost importance. I wasn't quite from the white glove set (although I did own a pair of elbow-length evening gloves once), but when I was a young woman, having matching shoes and handbag was a must. This meant my friends and I were usually late for work, because we had to stop and change purses every morning. And then we spent most of the day rummaging around in search of something that was at home in the other purse. But we looked really put together. Some women changed into comfortable low-heeled shoes when they got to the office, but always slipped the pumps back on when heading out again.

Then came the running shoes craze. I remember exactly when that hit Vancouver. The year was 1983. I worked for the PR agency, and one morning my colleague, a woman the same height as I am, with size 10 feet just like mine, arrived at the office wearing sneakers! Her feet looked huge and awkward. I was shocked. Mind you, after she took off her coat, she did change into fashionable footwear that perfectly accessorized her outfit, but I was stumped. She was doing it all backwards. Television newscasters were similarly mystified, running news stories of women's feet shod in big clunky runners walking up and down the city streets. From the ankles up they were all Ms. businesslike: suits, briefcases, fashionable purses, and so on. But the footwear! How could they? Soon though my own corns and calluses, developed from years of cramming my toes into uncomfortable high-heeled shoes, shouted out, "Lower your standards. Buy running shoes." And that's how I too joined the comfortable set and started wearing runners to work. I must admit, it felt much better.

Fast-forward to my new status as an Abbotsfordian. To get myself up and mobile first thing in the morning, I had started taking Duchess out for a "business" walk rather than just opening the door to the backyard for her. At 7:00 a.m., comfort and speed were crucial when I wasn't sure if I could get into street clothes before her need to go went. But, comfort and speed notwithstanding, I was inspired by a unique work of art that hung in our living room to upgrade my early morning look. Our friend Ebba Reiter is an extraordinarily talented artist whose attention to detail makes her subjects jump off the canvas. Ebba particularly loves to paint exotically dressed women from days gone by. Having worked for many years in the CBC Vancouver Design Department, latterly as manager, design and staging, she has the ability and talent to let loose her imagination on each painting.

Ebba Reiter, The Victorian Dog Walking Stick, acrylic on canvas 1989

A number of years before, Ebba had gifted us with a painting that she called *The Victorian Dog Walking Stick*. In it, a Victorian-era woman, dressed in a long flowing gown complete with bustle, an elaborate shawl, and elegant hat, is walking her three Lhasa Apso puppies on a very cold-looking moor. In her hand, the glamorous woman holds a large, ornate stick with a dog bone dangling from the end. In addition to admiring the imaginative detail comprising the woman's costume, and the unmistakable sense of cold that permeates the moor, the subtle humour dangling at the end of the walking stick elicited a chuckle every time I saw it. But, much as I admired this oil-on-canvas example of the fashionable way to exercise "man's best friend," it didn't quite work for me. Dragging a bustled gown through the wet grass en route to the barn was clearly a non-starter. Although I loved imagining myself in elaborate costumes from times gone by, especially one of those great hoop-skirted gowns from *Gone with the Wind*, practicality won out. I did however feel the need to create a dog-walking ensemble that was carefully colour coordinated and weather appropriate.

Ensemble in basic black, with emphasis on the long quilted coat, which not only keeps the dog walker warm, it also hides the pyjamas underneath. The black boots, black hat, and black gloves are set off by the use of spot colour around the neck—a blue and yellow scarf for warmth and a dash of flair. Duchess sports her regular black fur coat and red collar and nametag.

Ensemble for a wet day. Note the distinctive use of bright colours, perfect for visual impact. Key to the look is the coordinated use of waterproof black and yellow, with matching hat and jacket, and the black waterproof pants and boots. The yellow scarf adds that extra touch of warmth often needed when it's wet out. Duchess is seen here wearing her red collar and nametag.

One cold wet morning in early fall, I needed to throw fashion to the winds, literally. Outside, the weather was pouring rain and blowing up a storm. To fight the elements, I pushed stocking feet into my gum boots, zipped my long black quilted coat up to my neck, and pulled the hood strings tight around my face, leaving any accessorizing accoutrement at home. I was dry and warm and as scary looking as any Halloween prowler. In addition, I was carrying the fashion accessory par excellence. No dog walking excursion was complete without what we called in those parts the stall fork, a.k.a. long-handled pooper scooper. Carried jauntily over one's shoulder, *à la* the fishing rod of Huck Finn, the stall fork replaced our city friends' little plastic bags. A simple flick of the wrist into the nearby ditch, and ta-dah—poop all gone.

I sometimes wondered if the neighbours ran to cover their children's eyes when they saw my scary guise coming down the street. But I didn't much care about my appearance that day. Staying warm and dry was foremost in my mind. When I got back from my walk that particular day, Bill was up early and standing in the kitchen. He had the smallest hint of a twinkle in his eye, and he said, "When I was looking out the window just now … I saw … coming down the street—" The words to describe what he had seen weren't there. So I offered, "A vision in black?" We both burst out laughing and had a big hug.

* * *

When Matty and Kyle were younger, they didn't realize that Grampa Bill was having cognitive problems. Perhaps they thought everybody's grandfather was picked up at daycare and dropped off at home in the afternoon. And when they were at our house, they were more interested in playing with their toys or setting up a fort in the hayloft than in what their grandparents were doing. However, when their own abilities equalled and then surpassed Bill's, they did start to notice his behaviour was different from that of the other adults in the family. One day Matty's awareness of Bill's condition hit home and it really dazed me.

I had recently had the laundry room in the basement enlarged, a reno that required some major sorting and organizing of stuff into various piles: to toss, to send to the thrift store, to keep, and so on. The night before I had planned to deal with all the mess, Matty, now ten years old, had slept over, and first thing in the morning, he was gung-ho to help me in the basement. Bill indicated that he too would join the work party. So right after breakfast, I got Matty started sorting the pile we would take to the dump, and I asked Bill to move the stuff in the pile by the door out to the carport so we could take it to the thrift store. Nodding his okay, he picked up an item, and for the next two or three minutes, fiddled with it in his hands. Then he walked it out to the yard, brought it back, and put it back on the pile. For me, this was not a problem. He was keeping busy, which was one of my goals for him each day. But for Matty, Bill's behaviour was bizarre.

"I thought Grampa turned eighty last week," he said to me. "It seems like he's only two." I was caught off guard by his comment, and it upset me terribly. I told Matty that he was being disrespectful and suggested he go upstairs to his room and think about what he had said. A minute or two later, I realized Matty didn't really know *what* he had said. I knew Dianne had told both the boys that Grampa was old and couldn't do some things any more, but that we still had to be nice to him. What I didn't know was what else she had explained, or how much they understood. So I went up to talk to Matty. I didn't know what I was going to say—or where I would start. I just plunged in.

"If someone is sick with the flu, we don't make fun of them because they are throwing up," I started. "And we don't get mad at people who have a cold and are coughing so loud we can't hear the TV." I went on to explain that in those circumstances, we understand that the person can't help what they're doing. They have caught something—like a disease. "It's the same with Grampa," I said. "Only his disease isn't going to get better. He is sick in his mind. He can't think like he used to or talk like he used to. But we must still love him and give him the same respect and courtesy we did before."

I went on to tell Matty more about Grampa Bill—what he used to be like, that he was a talented actor, with roles on TV and radio and in movies. One of the TV shows he was in was the original *21 Jump Street*, with Johnny Depp. And I said he read books on tape for blind students so they could go to school and learn too. I hoped this broadened Matty's understanding of why Grampa Bill was like he was, and what he was like before he got sick. I could tell from his wide-eyed wonderment when I mentioned TV and movies that he was pretty impressed by his grandfather's career.

"He knows Johnny Depp?"

"Well, he used to, when Johnny Depp wasn't famous like he is now."

"That's cool!!"

Talking to Matty helped me as well as him. It was so easy to forget about the man who was stuck inside this new person walking around the house looking kind of lost. Amid helping him get dressed and getting him out for some exercise, organizing the routines of the household, and going to work, I didn't always have time to think about the really great guy I had married twenty-two years before. Arriving on the scene when Dianne was thirteen, he had survived not only her puberty but also my menopause. Now there was a guy with stamina. I'm not sure Bill ever knew what "normal" looked like, because by the time I came out the other side of night sweats and emotional outbursts, he had started sliding into dementia. But through all that, he was a great dad to my daughter and a wonderful husband and friend. He helped me start my own business and provided great support to his own dad and my parents as they declined. I was grateful to Matty for giving me the opportunity to focus on the man that I loved—the person who was still in there somewhere.

CHAPTER 10

Bring on retirement

ONE OF THE FIRST THINGS I discovered about autumn on the farm was the burn. When we moved from Vancouver, I asked about the messy pile of debris in the side field and Dianne said that was our burn pile. The previous owners couldn't take it with them, of course. So we got to burn their stuff as soon as open burning season started, on October 1. The next year, catching on to rural ways, we added to our own burn pile all summer in anticipation of the fall's giant bonfire. The accumulated flammable material comprised all manner of paper, empty chicken feed bags, and miscellaneous pieces of wood that collected around the farm. Anything burnable that we couldn't be bothered lugging to the dump went onto the burn pile. By the end of September, it was quite high.

Bill's glad we had accumulated enough stuff to make a bonfire

Sitting around the fire, hot dogs and drinks in hand, is a wonderful way to welcome the fall season

The weather over Thanksgiving weekend was sunny and warm, with a crisp feeling in the air and that undeniable scent of approaching autumn. So we organized a burn for Saturday night, bought hot dogs and all the fixings for s'mores, and invited friends of Dianne and Mike to come with their two kids, one a good friend of Matty and Kyle; the other his 11-year-old sister Amelia. Besides the hot dogs and s'mores that were cooked over the fire, the best part of the evening was sitting in lawn chairs beside the crackling blaze, watching the boys poke the flames with long sticks and then run to the nearby stream to put out their makeshift torches. Meanwhile Amelia ignored the boys and dreamily spent her time offering treats over the fence to Sassy and Cassidy, who had wandered over to see what all the fuss was about. Just as I was thinking to myself that city kids don't often get the chance to roast wieners over a fire or run with burning sticks, the young girl turned away from the horses and said to her mother, "This is the best Thanksgiving ever."

Along with Thanksgiving, creating new country-Christmas traditions was one of my great hopes for our move. That said, our first year, we didn't have a Christmas tree. As I've mentioned, we were still living in the basement suite, listening to contractors crash and bang above us as they brought the 1970s kitchen and bathrooms into the twenty-first century. We didn't see the point of decorating our temporary quarters, so that year we enjoyed the tree and decorations that Mike and Dianne and the boys had put up at their place.

But Christmases number two and three were another story. Call me Martha, but I was so excited to be living "out in the country" that I wanted everything we did to be old-fashioned/traditional. I called a girlfriend who baked and got recipes for plum pudding and Christmas cake. We bought a locally raised fresh turkey. Since our own vegetable garden had not been much of a success yet, we purchased all our Christmas veggies from the local market that specialized in high-quality organic produce. I did draw the line at churning my own butter, but I had purchased a giant canner in anticipation of creating shelves full of preserves. The canner, though, ended up storing water in the barn. Oh well. But as for the Christmas tree, no artificial or parking-lot tree would do. Christmas 2009, we were going to select our own tree right from the source.

Since neither Bill nor I had ever cut down a tree, we opted to visit a Christmas tree lot slightly off the beaten path where families have the choice to either cut their own tree or purchase an artfully cultured one that has been pruned to make any living room look totally "designer traditional." The day we chose for our outing could have been custom ordered for the occasion: clear, sunny, and cold, with just a sprinkling of snow on the ground. We picked up Matty and Kyle, who by this time were eight and seven, and made our way to Christmas wonderland. Carols and Santa songs were playing throughout the tree farm. The aroma of hot chocolate and apple cider mingled with the scents of pine and cedar boughs. Blow-up Santas made great props for pictures with the kids. While Bill and I selected just the right tree, the boys ran around the property checking out all the hot chocolate and candy cane stands. Then the four of us carried the perfect Tannenbaum to the four-wheel-drive van we had purchased a few months before and headed home, strains of Bing Crosby's "White Christmas" ringing in my head.

The next year we repeated the whole process, but with considerably different results. Weather on the day we chose to select a tree was pouring rain and windy. The cold blew right through us as we clambered out of the van. We had to hang onto our hats and scarves, and our coats were soaked through in minutes. The boys ran straight for the hot chocolate. Bill wasn't quite as into it as he had been the year before. I wasn't sure if this was because of the bad weather or if his dementia symptoms had ramped up that day. Given the circumstances, I made the fastest tree transaction ever. Is it green? Does it stand up? We'll take it. Then we played the senior citizen card, me just practicing how to be old, and had the young guys who worked at the lot carry that year's perfect Christmas tribute to our vehicle.

Christmas number four was the year I came to my senses and modified my Norman Rockwell fantasy. Early in December, when I was at the Co-op buying treats and grain for the horses, I saw that they had very real-looking artificial trees on sale for a terrific price. Remembering the rain pouring down my neck the previous year, I wanted to buy one of these trees but was worried what the boys would say. Would they miss our seasonal tradition of going out together to select the perfect tree? What would they think if we wimped out because the weather might be bad? So I invited them over after school that day, sat them down, and explained that we were thinking of getting an artificial tree, which would mean we wouldn't be going out to the Christmas tree lot this year...

"What do you think about that?" I asked.

Quick, shoot-from-the-hip response: "Can we still have hot chocolate?"

Immediate reply: "You bet!"

"Great."

Thus another, amended Nanny and Grampa tradition was born. Carry the tree up from the basement. Drink hot chocolate and eat candy canes in the living room. Stay warm and dry. How perfect is that? Later Mike and Dianne came over for a family decorating party. Much later I snuck out to the tree to rehang the icicles (a tradition that never changed).

* * *

January 2012 was uniquely special. On New Year's Day, I woke up a totally new person. Or at least, I had a totally new handle. I was no longer Pauline Buck, communications manager for the Kidney Foundation. My last day of work had been when the office closed for Christmas break. I was now Pauline Buck, retired, a.k.a. unemployed, out of work, house mouse and caregiver. Not only that, when my birthday arrived three weeks later, I was officially Pauline Buck, senior citizen. The weekend of my sixty-fifth, Dianne organized a birthday party complete with my favourite appies and wine. Guests included nearby neighbours, close friends Ebba and Bill Reiter (of CBC fame) from New Westminster, and Ben and Evy, who made a surprise visit from Victoria.

Now, where did I leave my bonbons?

Many people take this turning point in their lives hard. Myself, I was really excited, and so happy to be retired that at the party I wore my newly minted Gold Care Card around my neck for all to see. Fortunately, I didn't spill wine on it. Retirement meant so many new beginnings, and so much that I thought was going to be good. Starting with the fact that on January 3, I did not have to get in my car at oh-dark-hundred to beat the traffic into the city, then repeat the lengthy commute at the end of the workday. My life gained three hours each day. I felt younger already. And now I could see my grandsons more during the week—maybe pick them up from school sometimes and spoil them at Dairy Queen. In grandmother parlance, this is called revenge: get the kids hopped up on sugar, then send them home. I never said I would be a good person. Just a *retired* person.

But the most important aspect of being retired was that I could stay home and look after Bill all the time. I had felt bad leaving him with home care workers while I was at the office. Not that they weren't good with him, but I always felt he would be better with me. I'd felt the same way when leaving Dianne when she was young. For the first time in my life, I was getting to stay home and be with the person I loved. My vision was that Bill would continue to go to adult daycare twice a week, because he enjoyed the activities there and the friends he had made. And I would spend those two days pursuing my interests. I would see friends, work on the photography hobby I was hoping to pursue, and research how to organize my vegetable garden so it would produce carrots and tomatoes that were better than last year's. I also enrolled in a Weight Watchers program on one of Bill's daycare days. (That extra ten pounds was really hanging in there.) On non-daycare days, my plan was to organize interesting outings or activities if Bill was having a good day, or if not, just loaf around the house, at least till planting season started.

They say time flies when you're having fun. And they, whoever *they* are, were right, at least at first. I loved the freedom of retirement, not being a slave to the office routine. Whatever new routines I was planning, I could stay home to do them. Every morning when the clock radio turned on at the same time as it did when I was working, I would listen to the traffic reports, then smile and turn over in bed for a cuddle with Bill and a few more minutes of snoozing. Next, that rascal Duchess would start her take-me-out dance around the bedroom, so I'd get up and trek to the barn, with Duchess jumping along beside me, to let out the horses and chickens. En route back to the house, I would walk down the driveway to pick up the morning paper, checking to make sure none of the neighbours could see my pyjama bottoms hanging down beneath my barn coat.

Over my first cup of coffee, while Bill was still sleeping, I faced my initial challenge of the day—which items on my ever-growing to-do list would I tackle? The family room downstairs still needed a cleanout and cleanup. Stuff that hadn't been taken to the dump or thrift shop and had been temporarily shoved onto shelves still needed to find permanent homes. Those Royal Doulton "Top o' the Hill" figurines that my grandmother had collected continued to disdainfully turn up their petticoats at the electric screwdriver I had plunked next to them. Then there were a couple of half-full cans of paint, plus Matty and Kyle's toys that I kept rescuing from the floor so they wouldn't become puppy treats—all needing to be properly sorted and put away.

Or should today be the day I advanced on my home office? With tax season upon us, this seemed like the logical place to start. Also in need of immediate attention were the bedroom closet, the cupboard under the bathroom sink, and... Well, the list went on.

When I had been counting down the days before I retired, I had imagined myself as a whirling dervish, getting everything inside the house organized while the weather was still bad. Because I knew that when the sun came out and the days warmed up, I would become an instant outdoor person. Alas, my imagined activity spurt did not happen. My dervish seemed to need its batteries charged. The whirl was gone.

Over my second cup of coffee, I gave this conundrum a lot of thought and concluded that the problem was, there were no deadlines. I had worked to deadline all my life and fit the domestic necessities into the short space of time between coming home from work and going back to work. Now that there was no paid work, I could organize the family room any time I wanted. Same with the closets and under the sinks. Maybe tomorrow. Maybe not. Now, where did I leave my bonbons?

Within a couple of months, the novelty of being "free" in February's winter wonderland wore off. A person can only take so many art shots of snow howling around the barn or ice clumps hanging off the puppy's shaggy ears after a romp in the yard before the photography bug falls over on its back, lenses straight up. Cabin fever set in. Our big excitement was to venture out to Safeway to restock the pantry before the next scheduled freezing rain fell. Walking the dog became a treacherous task of *creeping* the dog down the icy road.

This was our fourth winter on the farm, and it seemed like the worst one. Maybe that was because winters two and three had been rainy and mild so I was out of the groove of a valley winter. Shovelling the snow wasn't a problem. Tim from downstairs did that. It was the ice that made me crazy. I had sprinkled so much salt in front of the house, I was sure the driveway would have a heart attack. And the depth of the snow out back! We had to shovel the chickens' fenced-in yard because they were snowed into their coop, as their outside door wouldn't open. The day my legs sank deeper into the backyard snow than the height of my calf-length boots, I started longing for spring. But the final straw came one garbage day.

Every other Wednesday, rain or shine, I dragged our two allotted bags of trash and an unlimited number of blue recycling bags out to the end of the driveway. When my friends asked me what I missed most about living in the city, I would say the condo's garbage chute. And I meant it. This one Wednesday morning, at 8:00 a.m., just before the truck was scheduled to come by, I slipped and skidded down the driveway, trailing my bags behind me. At noon, I saw that the bags were still where I had deposited them. Thinking the truck was just delayed, I didn't worry. But the garbage was still there the next day, and the next. When I asked Dianne, still our main source of country information, when she thought the truck would come, she laughed and said, "It won't. When they miss our scheduled day due to weather, or for any other reason, we don't see them again till the next official garbage pickup." Not only did we have to drag all the bags back in, now sodden from the snow and ripped open by who-knows-what, we also had to take them to the dump.

Yup, the novelty of country life in winter had definitely worn off. Even the three little snowmen in our neighbour's front yard were looking pretty sad—their carrot noses were either drooping listlessly or lying in a snowbank where the wind had blown them. Bring on the rain. Yikes. Did I say that out loud?

* * *

Aside from such inconveniences, caring for Bill full time turned out to be more difficult than I thought it would be. His dementia was taking more out of me than I had anticipated. When I quit work, I was ready to be Bill's caregiver, prepared to make sure he was up, showered, dressed, and fed and that we shared some form of exercise and fresh air, be that a walk with the dog, a trip out in the car, or a visit with friends. I knew it would be important to keep his mind engaged whenever possible and to keep things around the house cheerful. Hence I often tried to find a laugh or a joke in what was going on, because when people laugh together, they bond and their brains feel lighter. I suspect you won't find that definition of "humour for good health" in any medical books, but that was my philosophy.

For example, sometimes when Bill said something silly and I could tell by the sad look on his face that he knew he had just said something that made no sense, I'd say, "And you took your pills today when?" Then we'd both laugh and hug. To keep him feeling he was part of the household, I would ask him to empty the dishwasher and help set the table for dinner or put away the groceries. It didn't matter that he didn't do those chores well, or that after he went to bed I moved the dishes from the broom closet shelves to their proper cupboards. Such activities kept him busy.

Time to myself was limited to the two days a week that Bill attended adult daycare and a couple of hours in the afternoon when he was napping—time I used to do chores around the house, call a friend, or just sit and read my book. I was a big fan of fiction with a happy ending. Maeve Binchy was a favourite. Also I had the four weeks of respite care that Fraser Health provided for in-home caregivers every year, which certainly helped. So the physical routine was pretty well mapped out. But "knowing" something and living it were not always the same thing. It was the emotional toll that was affecting me the worst. And the continuing need for more and more patience, a trait that even Elaine, my best friend of almost fifty years, said I was always short of. But she said it with love—I think.

In health care speak, helping a person with dementia is called prompting them. Our case manager asked me how much prompting Bill needed. Initially I would remind him it was time to get ready for bed.

"Here are your pyjamas. Don't forget to clean your teeth." Standard stuff we parents did naturally years ago with our seven- and eight-year-olds. Then my prompting became "Here are your pyjamas. Take off your shoes. Let me help you take off your trousers. I'll hold the pyjama bottoms so you can step into them. This is your toothbrush. This is the toothpaste. Put the toothpaste on the brush… No, not on your finger—on the brush." And the prompting went on. Instead of progressing, my "seven-year-old" had regressed to becoming my "three-year-old."

All this prompting was part of the need for patience. But it also contributed to a sense of overall sadness I was feeling. Not just because it was necessary to show Bill how to clean his teeth, but because sometimes he just stood there, toothbrush in hand, staring at it like he was in some sort of trance. The thing that broke my heart was the absolutely defeated look he got on his face when he knew something had happened that wouldn't have under normal circumstances. Like the day he tried to make coffee by putting the metal coffee carafe on the stove and turning on the element. I had to call the fire department and ask them to come and check for toxic fumes in the house. This wasn't a bad thing though. I was glad to have our address in their records as a place where a person with dementia lived, in case of another emergency.

Besides all the prompting, I also found it difficult to figure out what we should do during the day. If I left Bill to his own devices after he was up and organized, he would fall asleep in a chair, which I thought was not good for him. He did like to have an official nap after lunch, and I counted on that time for myself, but it really bothered me that at any time during the day, he would just go to sleep. Should I just leave him in the chair sleeping? Or wake him up? A friend who had been the executive director of a long-term care home that served many residents with dementia told me that napping is not all that bad—and that people with dementia need more sleep. But surely not all day long! If I didn't include Bill in what I was doing when he was up, he would lie down. Then I'd feel guilty that he wasn't getting enough attention. We did have normal conversations sometimes—and discuss things. These weren't long talks, but we did communicate somewhat. I didn't want to lose that. So when he wasn't following me around the house, I was following him around, trying to amuse him or keep him involved. This was very tiring.

When my grandmother had developed dementia in her nineties, I remember that my mother was always mad at her. Nanny lived in a long-term care residence in Vancouver and was very well taken care of. But my mother could hardly stand to visit her. My grandmother knew it too. When she first lived there, Nanny and I used to talk about why Mom was always so short with her, or didn't pay any attention to her. They had been really close. My whole life I remembered Nanny and Mom having fun together. I finally figured out that Mom was upset that her "real" mother was going or gone, and this person who looked like her was all that was left. It was like my mother was in pre-loss mourning or anticipatory grief I think it's called. I was determined that Bill wouldn't go through that. My patience wore thin—sometimes more than I wished—but I would never be angry at Bill. Angry at his disease, yes. But it wasn't his fault.

One day, I was feeling particularly down. It was around 1:30 and neither of us was even dressed. I hadn't managed to get us organized. The house was a mess. We were sleeping in the spare room because I hadn't done the laundry and we were out of clean sheets. We'd been eating out of the freezer—hooray for leftovers—because I couldn't bring myself to make new meals. I was sitting at the computer in my home office deleting emails and trying to rustle up some interest in throwing in a load of laundry when Bill came in and stood looking at me—another thing he did all the time that bugged me. I said, probably in an exasperated tone of voice, "So what do *you* think we should do today?"

"Let's go to a movie." I was shocked at his response. "Really?" I said. "Yes" came right back at me. I sent him outside for the paper that I hadn't collected yet, looked up what movies were playing, and together we checked out a couple of films on the internet to decide what to see. Suddenly life felt back to normal. We both got ready—Bill with some prompting—and headed out for the 3:40 showing of *The Vow*, a romantic comedy inspired by true events that I highly recommend. What a nice ending that was to what had been a crummy few weeks. I felt my energy come rushing back. Suddenly the pile of laundry no longer looked like a monumental task and a grocery list started to form in my head. I realized this whole journey with Bill was going to be a series of ups and downs.

CHAPTER 11

Spring is in the air

In early spring I sent an email to friends from Uhill saying I wouldn't see them at church because I had to go to a Sunday afternoon seminar called Good Bugs and Bad Bugs, organized by Buckerfield's Farm Equipment and Nursery. After writing that note, I burst out laughing. Since when did I get all excited about garden bugs? It would appear the answer to that question was *now*. This was our fourth summer in Abbotsford. That in itself was shocking news—we'd been "farmers" for four years. And now that I was not dividing my time between home and work, I was bound and determined to produce a successful vegetable garden. Unfortunately, my attempts so far had been dismal failures. The previous year's weather had been so wet and miserable that even Craig Allison, host of NBC's series *The Carefree Gardener,* would have been hard pressed to grow bountiful produce. The carrot and bean seeds we planted had drowned, and the zucchini plants just turned to mush. And if you can't even grow zucchini, you're definitely a failure.

The year before that, we had a thriving crop of weeds that were well fed on the few veggies that did survive. Part of the problem was that I didn't know when the vegetables were ready. Take broccoli, for example. The plants came up and grew little broccoli-like flowers on the end of stems, but they didn't turn dark green. They never looked like what is in the store. So I waited … and waited … and waited. Next thing I knew, the broccoli had all gone to seed. Lettuce was another example. Who knew that the way to harvest lettuce is to pull the whole plant out, roots and dirt and all? That's why you plant lettuce often—in small amounts, so you can continue to harvest greens for the whole season. Not knowing that, I was gently picking off individual leaves and leaving the main plant to die. My single success that summer was tomatoes, which it seemed I was capable of nurturing. I had quite a few cherry and beefsteak tomato plants, all of which did well. I made tomato sandwiches that would be the hit of any local deli, and my Greek salads came to life with the cherry tomatoes. Thanksgiving Saturday was the day I chose to harvest my last remaining red tomato. It was at once a sad and tasty moment when I sliced into it and just ate it from the cutting board—not wanting to dilute its taste with lettuce and cucumbers.

Anyway, year four was to be *the* year. The tomato and bean seeds were in their little peat pods, the grow light was set up to encourage the first signs of life, the seed potatoes were waiting to be planted, and as soon as the warm weather came, we could put the carrot, peas, and other vegetable seeds directly into the ground. One of our plans was to plant runner beans in pots and grow them up the supports for the house's upper deck—pretty and practical. I also wanted to improve my herb garden. Needed more basil.

I'm ready. This year, Veggies R Us

Dianne was in on this with me, but I seemed to be the one most obsessed with the vegetable garden. Part of that enthusiasm probably came from being a newbie farmer. Plus, at that bug seminar I attended, I was horrified to learn that store-bought potatoes are sprayed at least four times before the truck brings them to the store. That did it for me. Safe home-grown food was the way to go. Around a dozen of us, some experienced cultivators, some neophytes like me, were gathered in one of the gardening sheds at Buckerfield's, listening to some interesting alternatives to spraying with pesticides. If aphids are feasting on your plants and flowers, bring on the ladybugs, we were told. Sold by the bagful at most gardening shops, ladybugs eat up aphids like crazy.

"Just sprinkle them out of the bag over the infested plant, and after just one day you will be aphid free," said the Buckerfield's expert. The trick, though, is you need to sprinkle more of those cute little red and black beetles for a few more days to finish off the aphid larvae. Dragonflies in your garden are also your friend, I learned. And if you see a praying mantis, don't kill it. It too is a good guy. That's assuming you know what a praying mantis looks like, of course. *Google probably has a photo.* There are alternatives to the "nasty" sprays if the all-natural ways to keep your plants healthy are not an option. Confer with the professionals. Before reaching for the toxic cans, think of your pet's health too. Licking their pads after running through sprayed grass or fields can make Fido or Fluffy pretty sick.

I was not about to buy a Pilgrim's hat or trade in my four-by-four for a buggy that Cassidy could pull, but I was still keen on eating, producing, (if I could) and purchasing food whose origins we knew all about. Since moving to the farm, we had been enjoying beef, lamb, and pork all raised nearby on grass we could see, and since Mike and Dianne started raising meat birds separate from the egg layers, our chicken dinners were local too. When I took Duchess for a walk, I realized I was watching my future barbecue steak dinner grazing quietly next door in Gerry's field. That took a bit of getting used to, but I soon overcame my uneasiness.

At the bug seminar I met Mary, a woman who soon became a wonderful and long-lasting friend. Believe it or not, we bonded over llama poo! During the question-and-answer portion of the presentation, I heard a voice from the back of the garden shed speak right up and ask, "Do you know where I can get some llama poo?" *What?* Many in the room chuckled, but others knew exactly what she was after. Mary was and still is an avid gardener, and she knew that llama poo is an excellent natural fertilizer. Trouble was, she lived in a suburban house on a city street—no llamas there.

"I actually have some," I offered. "I have a pile of the stuff behind my barn. You're welcome to it." As I said this, I thought to myself how popular I would be with the family, who'd have less manure to shovel to the larger poo pile. Mary could hardly wait to bring over her bucket and dig in. Amazing what turns people on. There was a lot I didn't know before attending that bug seminar.

*   *   *

Now that I had left behind the regular office grind, my morning routine took on an air of devil-may-care and fun. I didn't need to dress twice; once for home and once for the outside world. However, I still hid my pyjamas under boots and barn coat first thing. But I'd stopped worrying too much what the neighbours might think about serious bedhead. After plugging in the coffee maker on the way out the door, first stop for me and Duchess was the barn. In addition to the now-familiar routine of letting the horses and chickens out, I couldn't forget to give treats to Willow and Matteo, who were peeking around the corner of their shelter behind the barn. They were so amazingly cute that every morning I laughed out loud when I saw them. After tossing the hay in the corner holder for the horses, I gave Willow and Matteo their treats. People say that llamas spit if they aren't happy but ours never spat on us—or on our friends, who also enjoyed feeding them horse treats.

Once I was finished in the barn, coffee was starting to move up my wish list. But not for me quite yet. Duchess needed to check out the neighbourhood. Our street was half a mile long. So if I walked her from one end to the other and back I'd walked a mile. Making that trip morning and evening, I rationalized, was good enough exercise to allow an extra glass of wine at dinner while keeping the grape off my hips. Cesar Millan the "Dog Whisperer" says that when dogs sniff at stuff, it's like they're checking their email. Dianne and Mike's boys say the dogs are checking their pee-mail—sniffing to see who was there before and if they left any "messages." Since hearing this, I found myself wondering what drops of wisdom Duchess was picking up or leaving as we went. Of course, I checked out things too on our walk. I waved to my neighbours who were heading off to work (poor them) or taking their kids to school, and I stopped to talk to those who had come down their driveways to get their newspapers—some in outfits more outlandish than mine. I particularly loved waving to the neighbour who lived directly across the street. His morning getup was a knee-length black housecoat and slippers. When it was raining he added boots and an umbrella. All told, early morning was a very social time for me and Duchess.

* * *

One day in early spring, Bill got up much earlier than usual, which annoyed me slightly because he usually slept till 10:30 or 11:00, giving me time to do some of the stuff I liked to do. But it was a really nice day, so I suggested we go for a walk to Mill Lake Park, a local attraction we had visited before. That time of year, the pretty two-kilometre trail, which loops around the scenic lake, meanders through blossoming cherry trees and spring flowers. We had gotten ourselves ready, gathered up Duchess, and headed for the car when I saw that one of my tires was soft—verging on flat. First stop of the day: the closest gas station. The problem was, I didn't know how to put air in a tire. Bill had always done that, and before he was in my life, there were full-service gas stations. I did know how to put air in a bicycle tire, but had never needed to fill a car's tire. However, I knew it was crucial to put in only the correct amount of air. But how did you know how much air you needed or if you had put in enough?

When we were on the road, heading down Fraser Highway at a speed considerably slower than my usual, I said to Bill, "This is going to be a strange question, but do you think you can remember how to put air in a tire?"

"Sure," he said. *Hooray. He's having a good day.* When I asked him how you know how much air the tire needs, he said the air pressure was written on the tire. *Good news. We're set.* Turning into the first gas station we came to, I pulled up alongside the air pump as if I knew what I was doing and we both hopped out of the car. That was the end of Bill's good day. The air hose confused him. He couldn't get his head wrapped around the concept of putting the end of it on the tire's valve, even after I figured out to remove the cap. Then I tried. I pushed the tip of the hose onto the valve and depressed the lever. Lots of air noise, but I didn't have a clue whether any air was going in—or if too much was going in. And I was getting really frustrated.

About then I saw a man in a yellow safety vest walking across the far side of the gas station parking lot. I waved him over and asked for help, explaining that my husband had dementia and couldn't remember how to fill the tire, and that I didn't know how. To my relief, he was totally obliging. He showed me where on the tire the correct pressure (psi) was indicated, and he explained how the gauge pops up to indicate how much air is in the tire and how much more needs to be put in. While all this was happening, Bill was standing beside the air pump with the saddest expression on his face. He looked like the kid in the schoolyard who hadn't been picked for a team. I wanted to cry. After the man left, I said to Bill, "It's not your fault, you know, that you don't remember." To which he replied, "Then whose fault is it?" We just stood there for a few minutes, hugging in the middle of the gas station.

Twenty-four hours later, it was like the upset at the gas station hadn't happened. Spring was in the air. The sun was shining. The temperature was warm, and the family was at our house all day. My plan was to tidy up the lower deck out the back and hose it down in readiness for summer. After the family finished their barn chores at our place, they helped me get the deck space organized. The boys carried a winter's worth of old newspapers out to the burn pile and we planned a great bonfire for that night. I set out the fixings for a make-your-own-sandwich lunch—tuna, chopped egg, shrimp, and peanut butter—and we all sat on the upper deck for the first time that year, wearing only light jackets. While we basked in the sun at lunch, Mike and Dianne both got after me for not asking for help with the tire. I said I hated to bug them all the time and explained that even I sometimes forgot that Bill couldn't do things he used to do. Then when I couldn't do them either, I got upset. But I did promise them I would keep bugging them. And they said that was fine.

After lunch Dianne and I took a load of stuff to the dump and then hit the grocery store for the hot dogs and the makings for s'mores. While we were out Bill napped, and the boys stayed at our house to make sure he was okay. It was rather peculiar having your grandchildren "babysit" your husband. But it worked out well. They were old enough and I think they liked the responsibility. When Bill woke up, they kept an eye on him to make sure he didn't wander off or start doing something dangerous.

* * *

After a few months of retirement, I needed an attitudinal adjustment in the area of finances. When I retired in January, I thought that because I was home every day I could do everything—must have been a throwback to my "Super Mom" days in the'70s and '80s. I let my housecleaner go and told the gardener who had been cutting our lawn for the past two years that I would be doing it myself. I didn't want to spend any money.

I had budgeted on Bill and me being able to live on just our government cheques and the small RRIF deposits we'd arranged for when Bill turned sixty-nine. But expenses I hadn't planned for cropped up, sending my budget down the drain. Since losing the extended health benefits I had had through work, we were now paying for our own provincial health insurance and prescription drugs. Going to the dentist without extended health insurance was enough to make anyone cry, with or without the Novocain. In addition, now that we had been in the house for almost four years, things needed fixing. Our back stairs needed replacing. Some of the interior painting we had done when we moved in needed touching up. The screens on the windows, which had not been in great shape when we moved in, needed to be changed. Without realizing it, with such financial concerns, I began to feel frustrated all the time and overwhelmed.

Enter Philip, our wonderful financial adviser. He was the one who'd figured out how we could afford to buy the farm in the first place. Now I turned to him for ongoing advice. "You're not going to starve to death, you know, if you start drawing down some money each month from your retirement investments," he assured me. "You aren't millionaires, but you have enough to see you through. Your retirement years are what that money has been earmarked for." *Gotta love that man.* Next came Dianne, who reminded me I couldn't do everything in the house and still be available to meet the requirements that Bill's dementia presented on a daily basis. Dianne encouraged me to rehire the housecleaner and consider rehiring the gardener. So, cutting to the chase, the stairs got fixed, the interior painting was touched up, the screens got replaced, and the gardener came back. Peace of mind prevailed.

* * *

Spring is a wonderful time on a farm: longer days, budding signs of new growth, and new births. One evening in early May when Duchess and I were out for our after-dinner constitutional, I met my new neighbour, Ron, who was out enjoying the evening with his six-year-old grandson. He and his wife had bought the farm two doors down with their son and daughter-in-law, who had two darling little kids. Saying how much they were all enjoying rural life, Ron added that he was particularly excited about the experience this would be for his grandchildren. Ron and his wife had been brought up on farms in Saskatchewan, and they were happy to be back in a rural community. They were raising a few cattle on their property and as nature would have it, two calves had been born in the past few weeks. When the first calf arrived, Ron said his grandson immediately wanted to know whether it was a boy cow or a girl cow. Grampa said he didn't know yet. He wasn't close enough to see. Then the boy announced, "It's a girl. I can tell."

"Really? How?" asked his grandpa.

"Because I can see a long pink thing hanging down from her stomach."

I chuckled. "So, if it had been a long blue thing hanging down, it would have been a boy?"

"Of course," said the youngster and Ron and I both smiled broadly.

The domesticated newborns were all doing well too. The purebred standard poodle puppies that we had been handfeeding ten weeks before were fine, adorable, and in need of homes of their own. Dianne had them advertised on the social media site Kijiji. She didn't place the ad till the pups were eight weeks old and had been thoroughly vet checked to make sure they were all right. It was suspected a couple of them might be small for their breed, but all were healthy and lovable. Another litter was born at Dianne's place five weeks after the poodles. These puppies were goldendoodles. Mom was a golden retriever and Dad was Duke, Duchess's standard poodle mate. The pups were all fine, feeding from their mom and growing cuter by the day.

Willow with baby Grayson

Speaking of babies, Willow was a new mom! I was the one who discovered the minutes-old baby llama standing beside her mom, all wet and gooey looking, his spindly legs wiggling and wobbling as he mustered all the effort he could to stay upright. We had bred Willow eleven months before to a male from the farm she had been purchased from. As her delivery date drew close, we had moved her into the empty stall in the barn, which is where I discovered this wonderful little miracle while on my way to let the horses out one morning. Dashing to the phone we had previously installed in the barn for emergencies, I called Dianne to rush right over, then went back to admiring Mother Nature at work.

Researching llamas, Dianne and I were amazed to discover that baby llamas, which are called crias, are born with their mother in a standing position. The cria comes out and hits the ground, a high-risk method, one would think, to get the baby's breathing started. Llamas don't have long tongues so are unable to lick or dry off the filmy membrane covering their cria. For those living in captivity, their human handlers clean off the newborns with a dry towel, especially if the weather is cool. Unlike some animals, llamas don't eat the placenta. So Dianne and I buried it to avoid the attention of predators, after we were able to tear ourselves away from admiring our new family member. Dianne named him Grayson, and within a few days we spent much time leaning over the fence to watch him cavort around the field, running back and forth from his mom to Matteo, who seemed to love being "Uncle Matteo."

Mother Nature isn't always cute and wonderful, and Willow was not so lucky with her second pregnancy. We had been watching her belly grow and planning her move inside when, one morning, we noticed she was thin again. Where was the pregnancy? Where was the baby? For two hours we scoured the field that Willow and Matteo called home, looking for any sign of a newborn cria. In one patch of tall grass beside the fence we found what we thought might be the remains of the placenta. But no sign of the baby—dead or alive. We could only guess that Willow had given birth early and that a coyote had gotten into the field. Possibly the cria had died on impact with the ground during birth. Or possibly it was overwhelmed by an opportunistic coyote.

Another sign of spring on the farm was the need to restrict Cassidy's access to the grassy pasture. That time of year, ponies can't be put out 'til afternoon because the early grass is too rich for their systems. If they eat too much fresh grass they can founder, which means they could go lame. So every morning after I put Sassy out to the grassy field, I closed the gate, forcing Cassidy to stay in the sandy paddock 'til around two in the afternoon. Cassidy was quite choked about this and called loudly to Sassy over the fence every day. One morning Sassy decided to support her buddy by not heading right out to the side field. She hung around in the paddock and called back to Cassidy, who responded with quite a racket from her stall inside the barn. I was stuck. I couldn't let Cassidy out with Sassy right there, or Cassidy would make a break for the field. But Sassy wasn't budging. She wasn't heading into the field.

Fortunately, another of the lessons I had learned was that Sassy would do anything for grain. So all I had to do was put some grain in a bucket, take the bucket to where I needed her to be, in this case the grassy field, and shake it. Success! She came running through the paddock gate right on cue. I quickly closed the gate, let Cassidy out of the barn, and took a mental bow at my clever strategy. *Poor Cassidy. Some friend Sassy turned out to be.*

* * *

More and more, life on the farm was starting to resemble an emotional roller coaster. I never quite knew what each day would bring: More anxiety with Bill? Good times? Fun? Challenging weather conditions that disrupted plans to keep my spirits up? Every time I thought I'd attend to my garden it was pouring rain; every time I planned to accomplish something inside, the sun came out and I had to dash out to cut the grass before the rain returned. Jobs never seemed to get finished, and everything felt in a state of flux. Bill's dementia had taken a downward turn too and I had to keep a close eye on him more of the time, to make sure he stayed safe.

But a much-needed week of respite care in July helped. While Bill stayed in residence at Maplewood House, my girlfriend Elaine came over from Gabriola Island for a couple of days. I toured her around the neighbourhood, pointing out my grazing steak dinners next door. We sampled bottles from our reasonably well-stocked stash of wine in the family room downstairs and leafed through the Weight Watchers cookbook for appealing dinners. We chose meals with only a few "points" and carefully selected the low-fat vintages to pair with our culinary creations.

The real highlight that month was Matthew, who was now ten and a half. His dad had taught him all about the ride-on lawn mower: how to start it, drive it, and cut the grass properly. I'd never seen a happier or more proud-looking kid than Matty on that mower.

Matthew's first vehicle. And his first paying job

He instantly became my official lawn mower, and would call me a couple of times a week to see if my grass needed cutting. To see him sitting behind the steering wheel, expertly manoeuvring that machine around the trees, just missing the garden, made me feel very "verklempt," as Barbra Streisand would say. I paid him $5 a time and figured this setup would work till he turned sixteen and traded in the John Deere for a Henry Ford or some such alternative mode of travel.

Another positive development was getting to know Mary better, the friend I had met at Buckerfield's. After bonding over llama poo, we progressed to being dog-walking buddies, and then one day she turned out to be a very understanding sounding board. She lived with and looked after her elderly mother, and suddenly we both needed to vent about our similar situations. I had never said out loud that being Bill's caregiver made me feel angry and frustrated sometimes. And that I seemed to have used up the bag of patience I received at birth. Unbottling my feelings proved to be a healthy first start towards establishing some sort of mental balance in my life.

I also started attending educational sessions put on locally by the Alzheimer Society. The presenter was excellent, and thanks to a push from Dianne, I made an appointment with her to talk about how I was making out, which apparently wasn't as good as my out-in-public face would indicate. She helped alleviate the guilt I felt when I lost my patience with Bill, saying it was perfectly normal. She also encouraged me to work some time into my life for me—use Bill's two daycare days a week to socialize with friends, go to a movie, or cocoon at home, without feeling the need to accomplish something. She also told me that Dianne was worried about me. That meant a lot. I didn't know that.

One day I said in jest to a friend that I was feeling very Biblical. Every night, before going to bed, I had to wash my feet because they were so dirty that I wouldn't put them between the sheets. The spring weather that year was so bad that all my outdoor activity had me running around the property in farm boots that got very yucky inside. I mostly meant this as a joke, but then something else happened that made my foot washing joke not quite so funny.

I came out one morning and saw what looked like white fluffy stuff on the lawn, stuck to the grass. *Ah,* I said to myself, *manna from heaven.* Various pastors and Sunday school teachers would no doubt be pleased that something they had been saying over the years had stuck. But then I stopped and looked at the lawn again. The white stuff was just pockets of condensation looking like mist rising from the dew. The sun shining on it made the mist kind of shimmer, and suddenly I felt that it really *was* manna from heaven. I didn't feel so alone. It flashed in my head (or my heart?) that God had been working in my life again, sending help interspersed with moments of joy: a grandson who was now old enough to cut Nanny's grass; a new friend who encouraged me to open up; a push to talk to the experts about the challenges of being a caregiver; and an old friend who came to spend a few days walking alongside me during this difficult time. I guess I really was blessed. It just took dirty feet and the sheen of morning dew to make me remember that. Thanks be to God.

CHAPTER 12

Difficult days

IN AUGUST 2012, FOUR YEARS after we'd moved to the farm, Bill was admitted to hospital. He never came home again. The problem had started about six weeks earlier with an abscess on his gum that caused his face to swell so badly his left eye all but disappeared. This happened when he was staying at Maplewood House during one of my respite care weeks.

Because I was out of town, the staff at Maplewood called Dianne, who filled in for me when I wasn't available. She rushed Bill to the dentist, where his abscess was lanced and he was given a prescription that called for antibiotics to be administered intravenously at the hospital twice a day for three days, followed by an oral course of antibiotics for a week, to be given at home. While I was heading back on Friday evening, Maplewood called my cell to bring me up to date on what had transpired and to say that Dianne had taken Bill to the hospital that day for his first I/V treatment.

On Saturday I started transporting him to the hospital myself for his next two days of injections. I didn't bring him home from Maplewood in between I/V treatments until Monday because when I saw him Saturday, he was so weak he couldn't walk and could barely talk. He was in a wheelchair, and I needed help to transfer him in and out of the car, so I saw no sense in trying to deal with our stairs at home. By Sunday, however, his facial swelling was down, and Sunday evening he was walking on his own again and chatting to people we encountered in the hospital. Bill had the most amazing constitution. The IV nurse on Sunday night said to me, "Is that the same guy?" He came back home and the following Wednesday, I took him to the dentist for a root canal. Wednesday night I had expected him to be woozy from the anaesthetic and in pain when the freezing wore off, but remarkably he was fine. I thought he would spend Thursday in bed—a major trip to the dentist like that can really shake up your whole system. Not Bill. He was up by nine looking for breakfast!

Three weeks later, the real problems began. Bill had developed diarrhea and spent the day in bed sleeping. I tried to feed him some rice, which is binding, and gave him an over-the-counter remedy that didn't particularly help. About midnight he tried to get out of bed but had become so weak he couldn't stand up. I came around the bed to help him, but he just slid out of my arms onto the floor. Because I couldn't get him up myself, I called 911 to ask the paramedics to come and lift him back into bed. They did much more than that and probably saved his life. After taking his vitals, discovering he had a slight fever, and hearing his brief medical history of antibiotics and diarrhea, they recommended taking him to the hospital, "just in case he has a bit of an infection." It turned out that he was suffering from *C. difficile*, which is highly contagious and potentially fatal. *C. diff.* is a normal bacterium that lives in everyone's colon. For healthy people, it doesn't cause problems, but it can flare up in the gut of people with compromised immune systems, those who have been on antibiotic therapy, and the frail elderly. My guess is that the paramedics suspected *C. diff.* all along but didn't tell me so I wouldn't get upset.

You usually hear of people getting this infection *from* the hospital—not taking it *to* the hospital. Bill got it from taking antibiotics without also taking the natural bacterium *acidophilus* or probiotics. Since antibiotics kill all the bacteria in your system—the "bad" that the medication was prescribed for as well as the "good"— people taking antibiotics are at risk of developing diarrhea, which leads to dehydration, which can lead to the development of *C. difficile.* I did not know this at the time. Bill developed *C. diff.* at home after being on antibiotics for two weeks and not taking any kind of probiotic. Had I known to even feed him probiotic yogurt, or any of the probiotic pills that are available without a prescription at the pharmacy, everything that followed might have been avoided. I was absolutely incensed to learn that this life-threatening and highly contagious disease can be so easily prevented. All doctors, dentists, and pharmacists should tell patients and clients to include probiotics in their diet following a course of antibiotics.

For his first two days at the hospital, Bill was totally out of it—sleeping day and night, including right through his eighty-first birthday. Not eating because the nurse couldn't wake him up to feed him, he was initially on a saline drip for his dehydration while the doctor waited for the lab tests to see if he did indeed have *C. diff.* When the diagnosis came in, he was immediately started on oral antibiotics and placed in isolation. *Great,* I thought. *More antibiotics!* All visitors and hospital staff were required to gown up before going into his room. Next came the diagnosis of another infection that showed up in the blood tests, and he was put on yet another IV antibiotic. My worry, of course, was that the *C. diff.* would kill him. (We had lost a friend around Bill's age a few years back to *C. diff.*, acquired in the hospital.) Looking at Bill lying there, so weak and pale, he seemed to be gone already. *Is this it? Is this how he is going to go?*

Secretly, I thought it wouldn't be a bad thing if the infection took him. Bill's quality of life had diminished terribly, and seemingly quite suddenly in the previous month—at home he slept most of the time and he'd become unsteady on his feet, which was new. He hadn't fallen, but I'd been keeping a close eye on him, especially near the stairs. Now he could barely speak, and when he did, what he said didn't make much sense. Occasionally out popped a sentence that was relevant—but not often. I had been thinking of making an appointment with our case manager to discuss the possibility of getting him into long-term care. But I'd been really dragging my feet. The thought of putting Bill into a home was breaking my heart. How could I put him in the car, drive him there, and never pick him up again? It would be like taking your kid to boarding school and never coming back to take them home. Then I would think, *If he's in a home, who would kiss him good night?* and I would start to cry. In addition, I had quite a hang-up about "nursing homes" because in the early 1990s, my mother had been in such a bad one in Vancouver and I couldn't get her to agree to move. Hers had that urine smell that made me want to gag every time I entered, and the amenities were minimal at best. I kept thinking of Bill in a horrible place like that and just couldn't take the step. Finally Dianne convinced me to tour some nursing homes in Abbotsford, and I discovered they were quite nice.

With the *C. diff.* finally gone, one day I went to visit the hospital and found Bill sitting up in a wheelchair out in the hall. He was sound asleep, mind you, but sitting up, which was good. A few days before that he would not have been able to hold himself up. While I was there, the physio came along and got him standing and walking the halls. I was relieved to see him looking so much better. One of my worries was that he would never get his strength back because he wasn't eating, so I would take him homemade soup because the liquids the hospital gave him were almost tasteless. But he must have had some internal fortitude that was bringing him around in spite of having so little to eat.

Unfortunately, Bill's rally was short-lived. He developed a blood clot that caused swelling in his right foot, and another infection surfaced, for which he was prescribed yet another antibiotic. When I insisted the hospital give him *acidophilus* to combat the antibiotics, the nurse was quite puzzled by this and said she would ask the doctor to order it. She had never heard of taking it as a precaution! Yet Bill might not be going through everything he was going through if I had known to give him *acidophilus* in the first place.

After about three weeks, when all these infections had cleared up, I had started to realize that Bill probably wouldn't be coming home. He was still too weak to walk, and I knew I couldn't physically move him in and out of a wheelchair. His dementia symptoms had skyrocketed because of all the confusion of being in hospital. A social worker who had been assigned to our case (I hated thinking of us as being a "case") told me that when he was well enough, Bill would be released to a care facility. I knew he wasn't at death's door any more, which eased my mind, but I was also in mourning about this next and last stage of his life.

A day or so after speaking to the social worker, I drove down to Lynden, Washington, with Dianne to pick up something for her horse that she had ordered online. After getting her parcel, we went to the restaurant next door to the UPS place for a snack. As we walked through the front door, I remembered that Bill and I had been there once to get something for Dianne and had gone to the same restaurant. Then I got that sinking feeling, knowing that Bill and I were not going to be back to this place again. Well, we probably weren't going to be *any* place together again, I realized, and the lump that seemed to live permanently in my throat grew a bit larger.

* * *

Thanksgiving that year was different. The weekend activities were normal, as this was our time to attack lots of the pre-winter prep. But there was no Bill in the house. He was still in hospital, and plans were under way to move him into long-term care when a bed became available.

With the barn needs of two farms to tend to, Mike and Dianne had become good at organizing their time and their to-do lists for all of us. On Saturday, the family came over, tools and wheelbarrows in tow, for a daylong work bee. On Sunday, we finished up a few things and then sat down to Thanksgiving dinner. We were a small and slightly subdued group around the table—just Mike and Dianne, the two boys, and me. While Bill wasn't there in person, he was with us in spirit. Usually I was the person who said grace at special family meals. This year, however, I asked everyone around the table to say what they were thankful for. We all mentioned our gratitude for the usual list of blessings: great weather; delicious food, the ability to live on a farm property and enjoy all that entails. The boys surprised the adults when they each, in their own way, said they were thankful to live in Canada.

I said I was thankful that Bill was being so well taken care of by the staff at the Abbotsford hospital, especially the care aides. When they saw me coming, they would stop to tell me how Bill was doing—how much he had eaten of his recent meal; whether he was out in the hall in his wheelchair to get a change of scenery from his room. I was also thankful for my friends and family who were being so supportive with their phone calls, emails, and so on. And, at the risk of sounding smug, I was especially thankful for the publicly funded health care system in Canada. It ain't perfect, but Bill had been in an awfully expensive hospital bed for over a month, receiving care, tests, and meds, running up costs that outside Canada would bankrupt anyone but Jimmy Pattison, BC's local billionaire. I said I would happily keep paying my taxes. Although I knew I would now be living on my own, I hadn't yet done any serious thinking about what life would look like, being too focused on dealing with the present. If asked, I knew that I did plan to stay in the house, but after that, who knew?

* * *

Much as I had fought against it, after his six-week stay in hospital, there was no question. I could not bring Bill home. He couldn't stand, walk, or feed himself. The hospital care aides used an overhead lift to move him from his bed to a wheelchair. When a bed became available 15 minutes away from the farm at Bevan Lodge, a long-term care facility owned by Trillium Communities, I was told that was where Bill would be going. Bill qualified for a government-subsidized room, which meant he paid only 80 percent of his after-tax income for long-term care services. That also meant we were obliged to move to the first publicly subsidized facility where a vacancy came up. Fortunately, Bevan was an attractive place with a friendly and caring staff. The lobby of the three-storey building was decorated tastefully, and the private rooms were small but comfortable. Families were encouraged to bring in wall hangings and pictures to personalize each resident's space. This also gave the care aides a better sense of the residents' lives.

In addition, Bevan had a great chef. The food there was delicious. I would plan my visits around mealtimes, which gave me something to talk to Bill about as we sat in the dining room with his tablemates. Visiting at mealtime also enabled me to sample the fare. Sometimes I'd call ahead and order myself a plate for a very reasonable price. Sometimes I'd nibble off Bill's plate. I called it "quality control." Actually, I was just avoiding the need to go home and eat alone.

One day I found myself, at three in the afternoon, eating a peanut butter sandwich and drinking a glass of milk at my kitchen counter at home. I called it lunch because I hadn't eaten since breakfast, except for the ice cream Bill had shared with me at noon. I had arrived at Bevan just a bit too late to "share" the fish and chips they were having but boy, the aroma in the dining room sure woke up my taste buds. The best meal of all, however, was one Sunday night's dinner that featured roast beef, Yorkshire pudding, mashed potatoes, gravy, vegetables, and for dessert, a homemade peach pie. Not knowing what was on the menu that night, I hadn't called ahead for a dinner of my own, but I did get there with enough time to share Bill's. Unfortunately, I didn't get much of a chance, as Bill inhaled his meal too fast for me to perform my "quality control" role.

One of the first arrangements I made when Bill moved to Bevan was for a physiotherapist to work with him two or three times a week to get his strength back. It didn't take long for him to be out of the wheelchair, using a walker on his own and, when the physio was there, walking the hall a short distance unaided. My hope was that his strength would return completely.

Before he developed dementia, Bill was always a friendly person—easy to get along with and cheerful. That part of his personality did not change, and it was no time at all before everyone on his floor knew and liked him—well, the staff anyway. It was hard to know how much the other residents knew or who they liked. I don't think Bill understood where he was, and by then I wasn't sure whether he knew who I was when I visited, and as usual, I was afraid to ask. Bruce, one of Bill's very close friends, called me one day to apologize. He said he would like to visit Bill at Bevan but he couldn't go. His exact words were, "I'm a coward. I can't stand the thought of seeing Bill there." I wondered if I was a coward too. Should I have tried to find out or figure out what Bill understood about what was happening or what had happened to him? I honestly didn't know, but he seemed to be at peace with his new life. I never offered to bring him home for a visit or a special occasion, because I was afraid he wouldn't want to leave again, and what would I do then?

I seemed to be a person who avoided situations I didn't want to know about—not sure if that was new or if I'd always been like that. But for me, it was easier not to think about how much Bill understood. Just go with the flow. Did that make me a bad person? I didn't know the answer to that question either. When I visited Bill, I tried to connect—to spend some quality time with him, even if we were just sitting saying nothing. I liked to give him a head and neck massage—upper back too. He seemed to enjoy this as well. Physical contact was important for us both, and a bit of a massage is welcomed by people in wheelchairs.

After lunch one day, Bill and I went downstairs to the lounge to hear a group of singers. There were about eighteen men and women in the group, all seniors themselves, dressed in attractive black and white: black vests, white blouses or shirts for the women, and bow ties for the men. They came regularly to entertain. That day, accompanied by their pianist, they presented their Remembrance Day concert, music that was much loved by the twenty-five or so residents in the audience—even by those nodding off. For some reason during their show, I started to get really emotional. Their selections were vintage World War II: "The White Cliffs of Dover," "We'll Meet Again," "Lili Marlene," and others. The songs were so meaningful to those listening that I began to well up too. The music was meaningful to me as well. Not that I was around during the war, but my parents were, and I grew up knowing those songs. Maybe while the others in the room were missing their buddies or sweethearts, I was missing my parents. I think I must have also been missing Bill. We were sitting side by side, and we were holding hands, but I was still missing him. I don't want to suggest we had a marriage made in heaven or to put him up on a giant pedestal. But it was heartbreaking that his rich CBC voice was reduced to just a whisper, his former purposeful gait was now a mere shuffle behind a walker, and his ability to recognize Bill and Ebba Reiter, the one pair of good friends who did come to visit, was gone. But all was not lost. He was still the gentle soul that everyone always loved.

This whole aging business gives me the pip, to use a British expression I had picked up along the way: the need to live in a care home, the loss of one's faculties, requiring help to dress and bathe, sleeping midday in a wheelchair during a planned activity, waiting for a care aide to come along and feed you. When Bill still lived at home and I came in and out of Maplewood House on his twice-weekly daycare days, I would turn my head away from the people sleeping in wheelchairs who lived there. I didn't want to see them. I didn't want Bill to become one of them. Now he had. But it's amazing how our perspective changes when we're right in the middle of a situation.

After just two weeks of visiting Bill at Bevan, I started to know some of the residents and their families. One man came every day to feed his wife her lunch. He was in his mid-eighties himself and lived in an apartment fairly close by. His wife was very frail and didn't talk much, but she knew him and responded to things going on around her. Another resident had moved in only a week after Bill. He used a walker but was mobile and quite independent. On the way back up in the elevator from the entertainment that day, he told me his wife had died from cancer three weeks before and he had cared for her until the end. Then he had moved to Bevan. "I had no place else to go," he said as his eyes teared up. Mine did too. The night of the roast beef dinner, one of our tablemates, a dignified and well-dressed woman, asked me for her purse. "I'm ready to go back to my room now," she said. "Who should I pay for this delicious dinner?" I can still see her well-styled silver-grey hair and the lovely pink cardigan she was wearing over her dress. Not wanting to confuse her more, I assured her, "There is no charge tonight. You're a guest." "Oh, thank you so much," she graciously replied with a smile. Then she proceeded to ask every care aide that went by the same question: "Who should I pay?"

What am I saying here? I used to equate long-term care homes with something ugly out of Dickens. So whenever anyone asked how long I would keep looking after Bill myself, my response was always "Always." Well, elder care has come a long way since the Victorian era. And I guess I too had come a long way since I had shied away, back at Maplewood, from real people with real lives who just needed help to live the best they could, with dignity.

* * *

"I like it here." These words made my heart sing when I was visiting Bill a couple of weeks after he had moved into Bevan. I had been worried that he might be unhappy, or agitated, or feel deserted living in a long-term care facility. I also wondered how he felt when I came to visit. And when I left. I had been studiously avoiding the word "home" in any conversations I initiated, which left me with little to talk about at all, and that bothered me too. I was getting depressed, feeling guilty, and was sad all the time about the fact that Bill had dementia and was living in long-term care. At that point I realized I needed some professional help, so I called Beverley Pugh, the counsellor who had been so helpful twenty-five years before when Bill and I were working out the "kinks" in our relationship. Now I hoped she would be available to help again.

"You may not remember me, but…" were my opening words when she answered the phone, and I was delighted and amazed at her response. "Of course I remember you. And how's our Bill?" She had really liked Bill in our long-ago sessions. I secretly think she worried for him in his new arrangement. Suddenly living with two females, regularly flashing their hormones, can be quite a culture shock. I filled her in on Bill's dementia and my concerns for him as well as for myself. An hour later, I had jotted down a pile of notes, gone through a box of tissues, and felt relieved and guilt free. Among other things, she explained that for people with dementia, their spirit is in transition. The physical person is still there but their spirit is moving on. She advised that when I visited Bill, I did not need to be chatty or cute or make idle conversation. Rather, I should sit quietly beside him and let his spirit and mine do their own thing—commune together, as it were. He might talk about things on his mind that might not make any sense to me, but they did to him, so I should just go along with the conversation. She also said to hold hands, because physical contact was important for us both, and it's crucial for people with dementia to know they are loved. Above all, I shouldn't feel guilty or bad—Bill was fine. He was just in a different place.

Following her advice made my visits much easier. I didn't have to worry about what I would talk about. Maybe this new approach to visiting was easier for Bill too. He didn't have to try to relate to what I was saying or try to remember irrelevant things like what he had had for breakfast. So after initial greetings and a time of orientation while he adjusted to having me there, we just sat quietly. One day, while we were sitting together, he suddenly said, "I like it here. I've met some nice people." Thankfully I didn't burst into tears on the spot. I waited till I got back in the car to do that. I simply said, "That's nice. I'm glad," and we sat there for a while longer.

* * *

One December morning, after Bill had been living at Bevan for a couple of months, the kid in me jumped for joy when I opened the bedroom drapes and saw that it was snowing. Not that I wanted to rush out and build a snowman or invite the grandkids over for a snowball fight. *Au contraire, mon ami.* I was excited because I didn't care that it was snowing. I wasn't at all bothered by those artistically perfect little white flakes that can so quickly develop into a mound of white treachery, wreaking havoc on roads, sidewalks, and roofs. This winter I didn't have to drive on a bridge or commute to an office. I was still in year one of being a retired boomer and was still loving all the stay-at-home perks of being out of the workforce. Plus I didn't even have to shovel the stuff. Yay, Tim.

The snow did conjure up thoughts of Christmas though, and family gatherings. Perhaps all those Currier and Ives cards were responsible, with the old-fashioned pastoral scenes or families gathered around a holiday feast. The traditions pictured in Hallmark cards don't always depict today's reality, but they do serve to remind us of some of the more important aspects of life. Whatever is celebrated every December; whatever customs are honoured—be they for Christmas, Hanukkah, the winter solstice, or just the chance for a midwinter holiday—it's good to set aside time to gather with friends and family and share the love that is often taken for granted throughout the year.

On Christmas morning 2012, I walked alone down the street, presents in hand, a single pair of footsteps crunching in the snow. If I had been able to bring Bill home, or even if I had been inclined to do so, the busyness of the day would have been too confusing for him. The previous year, before he moved to Bevan, he had been overwhelmed with all the activity in the house and spent much of the day napping on the couch. My big sadness for this year was initially that he wouldn't be with us at dinner. Five of us would be at our family table and one of us would be at Bevan, eating Christmas dinner with tablemates—virtual strangers. Then I heard that Bevan offered families the opportunity to have dinner there, in a private room, so everyone could be together. When I mentioned this to Dianne, she instantly said, "Great—let's do it." So Christmas morning we had our usual under-the-tree gift giving followed by our traditional eggs Benedict brunch accompanied by champagne mimosas, and the Merry Christmas phone call to Carol and Dan in Summerland. But in the afternoon, instead of dashing around the kitchen making last-minute preparations for a turkey dinner, we relaxed and played board games with the kids. Around four we headed to Bevan with Bill's gifts, white wine, and snacks of cheese and crackers tucked under our arms. We trooped up to his third-floor room and ceremoniously wheeled Bill down to the guest dining room on the main floor, where we all were glad for the chance to be together. Bill seemed to be enjoying himself too, but I wasn't sure if he really understood everything that was happening.

Family Christmas dinner with Bill at Bevan

Before dinner, he opened his gifts, with a bit of help from me—okay, the boys pitched in too to rip off the wrapping. The adults shared the bottle of wine along with appies, and just as the cheese ran out, the server arrived with our steaming plates of roast turkey, mashed potatoes, gravy, dressing, and good old Brussels sprouts. For dessert there was tiramisù! The chef had outdone himself. No Christmas feast could have been better than that. It felt so good that we had been able to have Bill with us during this part of Christmas rather than leaving him with strangers the whole day. And we loved it that our new Christmas dinner plan didn't come with any dishes to wash. As for left-over turkey sandwiches, who needs 'em?

* * *

To help fill in long days on my own, I took up bridge. Again. I had played this card game a number of years before, but never quite mastered it. Although I liked the game a lot, I'd never progressed to the point where I could say with any confidence, "Yes, I play bridge." Like tennis, the most honest answer I had when asked whether I played was, "Yes, I play *at* it." When one of the women in my Weight Watchers group suggested starting a bridge club and offered to teach anyone wanting to learn, I jumped at the chance. Two others were in too. Soon every Tuesday afternoon, members of the fledgling WW bridge club alternated homes and worked on our game. I absolutely loved our time together. Not only was I now learning to play properly, but I was also studying—at night, in bed. I'd exchanged my collection of Maeve Binchy novels for a series of beginners' bridge booklets and would fall asleep memorizing how many points were needed to open the bidding, how many points to respond to my partner, and for heaven's sake, to *never* trump your partner's ace.

Well, just as I thought I could return to some light reading, ten-year-old Kyle put the kibosh on that plan.

"Nanny," he said right after dinner and before his sleepover reached popcorn time.

"Yes, sweetheart."

"When I was downstairs, I saw a chessboard set up on the shelf beside the freezer. Do you play chess?" Somehow I knew I was doomed.

"No, honey, I never have. That's Grampa Bill's chessboard. I don't know where it came from or when he ever played. Never with me. Must have been before we met. But it's a nice one, so I just keep it set up. Maybe one day I'll learn." *Big mistake.*

When I first became a grandmother, I was excited about the fun I would have with my first grandson, Matthew. We would hug a lot. We would play. I would show him which Fisher-Price toy goes in which slot and how to fish out Cheerios from the plastic container at snack time. When he asked me something, I would know all the answers. When his brother Kyle arrived eighteen months later, I had grandmother bliss in duplicate, which became even more perfect after Bill and I moved down the street from the boys. Together we baked cookies, rode bikes, and selected the perfect Christmas tree. They stayed overnight. We made popcorn. And when they asked me questions, I knew the answers. Grandmotherhood was perfect. I was a wiz. I could do no wrong.

Then my grandsons started to display signs of being really smart. Their questions got harder, and my status as the "with-it" grandmother who knows everything began to slip. Soon the first signs of tech talk started creeping into their vocabulary, and before I knew it, I was miles behind. They would come over, shout "Hi," and dash into my office to play on my computer. They were logged into the internet and before I could give any thought to changing my password, they were happily blowing up "the enemy" in their online games. Oh, Fisher-Price, where art thou now? I must say, though, that their parents were extremely strict. The boys were only allowed on a couple of sites. And they stuck to the rules. I checked regularly, pretending that I knew what I was looking at. And I secretly hoped I could have known more than they did for a little longer.

I had heard that grandparents should teach their grandchildren how to play cribbage, so the kids would come to visit them when they were old. On the night that chess entered my life, I remembered that advice and applied it to that game. Of course, not knowing how to play did not deter me. We had a book. I figured Kyle and I would learn together. What fun. Kyle said he knew how to play, but most preteens exaggerate about what they can do and most adults ignore their claims. That night, I ignored his claims to my peril. The kid had played before. He knew how the chess pieces moved: which ones go only sideways, which ones go forwards and sideways, which can go forwards but only take out an opponent on an angle, and so on. The rules of chess made bridge decisions about whether to bid two hearts or two spades a snap. And thanks to setting up online battles and taking out enemy fighters ad infinitum, Kyle also knew how to strategize his moves. So there I was, madly flipping through the chess book for guidance. After minutes of mental gymnastics, book reading, and head scratching, I confirmed that my man, a.k.a. my Bishop, could indeed progress diagonally and I made my move. One second later, Kyle swooped in with his Knight and took out my King, my Queen, and my Bishop!

So that night I found myself sitting up in bed studying chess! Maeve Binchy was back on the shelf. If I were ever going to keep up with Kyle, I knew I'd have to stay on my toes. But how much bedtime cramming time did I have left before I was old? And I didn't even know how to play crib! Not to worry. So far, despite my shortcomings as a chess player, Kyle still loved me.

* * *

I do love Valentine's Day—always have. For Bill's first Valentine's Day at Bevan, I thought it would be fun to have a celebration with him. Even if he didn't fully understand what the day represented, I did. I made him a card with a weird-looking stick person on the front and a caption that said, "My Funny Valentine." Inside was a picture of the two of us laughing. I smuggled in a split of champagne, two glasses, and some chocolates, and we had those in his room, sitting in front of his window with bright winter sunshine beaming in on us.

Early one morning, when I opened my front door, I heard birds chirping for the first time in months. Spring must be just around the corner. Hearing nature's springtime chorus was one of the things I loved about living in the country. I had probably noticed the birds singing when we lived in the city, but not as clearly. Here there were no motorcycles barrelling up and down our road or sirens screeching through the traffic to block the music. Duchess and I trotted down the street for our before-breakfast walk with zest in our step, me thinking about warm sunny days ahead. When we got back, I realized my house was the only one with the outside lights still on. Time to set the timer to turn off sooner. These signs of spring were welcome because some days I felt mired in the mental slush of winter, yet other times I was full of vim and vigour. Go figure, as the kids would say.

Much had changed and I wondered what was coming next. Looking back on the previous year, I had first become a bona fide senior citizen and a retired person. I had embarked on a new volunteer position as Bill's full-time caregiver, watching with alarm as his dementia worsened. I had started to do some freelance writing. And during the early fall, I'd visited Bill in hospital for six weeks and then resigned myself to the fact that he needed to move into long-term care. By mid-November I was all alone in the house. It was a mixed blessing to have the house to myself and to call my days my own. I felt delight that I could come and go at will. I didn't have to plan for someone to come in and sit with Bill so I could go out, or take him with me to various appointments. Although he had been the darling of the hairdressers, and staff at the spa were still asking about him after I arranged one day for us to get a pedicure together rather than expecting him to just sit and wait in the lobby.

But, given the complicated emotions that accompany caregiving, I also felt guilty that I felt delight. And I often felt lonely—especially during the evenings. I was lonely before Bill moved into Bevan because we didn't communicate much and didn't do much, but at least there was someone in the house. Now I talked to Duchess, which was better than talking to myself out loud, but not much. Silent evenings, when I would sit with a glass of wine in front of the fireplace, became a time of personal reflection. Looking back over the past sixty-six years, I realized I had been blessed with an amazing variety of experiences, including opportunities to travel. I had met many interesting people and made a few close friends, enjoyed a varied and reasonably worthwhile career, and become part of a nurturing and fulfilling faith community. I loved and was loved by my small but mighty family, plus eight first cousins scattered across the country and various out-relations. I also loved and had been well loved by Bill. But now what?

Early that January I had attended the funeral of a friend. One of the readings at his service was from the book of Ecclesiastes—that well-known passage in chapter 3 that says, "To everything there is a season, and a time to every purpose under the heaven." It goes on to list "A time to be born, and a time to die; A time to plant, and a time to pluck up that which is planted;… A time to weep, and a time to laugh; A time to mourn, and a time to dance." And there's more. I suspect these verses are read a lot at funerals. The passage is quite fitting. But as the rabbi read these words of comfort, it occurred to me that what was missing was "a time to move forward." Maybe a funeral would be too soon for mourners to hear that advice, but for me the timing was right.

It was time for me to move forward—to think about my next steps. On occasion I experienced a fair degree of excitement about what might be in store for me, although the excitement came and went. I concluded that the trick was to be patient, to wait and watch for opportunities. At times I moved past some of the guilt I had felt when anticipation sprang up about starting a new life. But I didn't move past the sadness about Bill's condition. I'd always sensed that there was a purpose for my life, that there was some way I could contribute positively to those around me, but I could never quite put my finger on what that purpose was. Obviously I wasn't destined to be the world's next Nobel-winning scientist or the person to bring about world peace. But on a smaller scale, I looked forward to discovering what I would or could do locally for the next twenty-five years. *Note to self: Remind the financial advisor of my plan to live to ninety-five.*

* * *

I've already mentioned that when we first moved to the farm, I was quite offended by the presence of the poo pile behind the barn. I was glad I could ignore it most of the time. But every three or four weeks, on clean-the-chicken-coop day, I had to face my rural nemesis. In the beginning I was squeamish about taking a turn to push the wheelbarrow full of chicken droppings up that mountain of not-quite compost. *Walk on that stuff? Not this city slicker. What if I slip? What if I fall down in it?* No amount of "job well done" or warm cinnamon buns would make up for the degradation that sitting in a pile of horse and chicken poo would cause. For the most part, Mike or the boys took the wheelbarrow, but after a while I started taking turns too, not wanting to be a sissy.

Over time, though, I became adept at this job and, dare I say, amazingly cavalier about marching up the mound and depositing my load. Actually, I got downright smug about the whole thing. Sometimes, while cresting the peak of the pile, I would think how clever I was. How flexible. How versatile. I told one of my city friends once that I had become so adaptable I could fling hay to the horses at dawn, scoop chicken poop into a wheelbarrow mid-morning, then exchange my work boots for a pair of designer shoes and drive into town for a lovely lunch in a trendy restaurant. How adaptable is that?

Then came my fall from grace. *What ghastly weather for chicken coop day*, I thought when I woke up to monsoon rain on the farm that fateful Saturday. But, cinnamon buns at the ready, I climbed into my boots and farm coat and headed out to meet the family, rain dripping down my face even before I reached the barn. Forty-five minutes later, during the last run up the hill, it happened. I was just thinking one more time how good I was at this job now when my foot slipped and down I went, dignity first, into a pile of chicken and horse you-know-what. I found myself sitting up to my armpits, bum down, legs splayed out in front, hands straight up in the air. I didn't know whether to laugh or cry. Of course, Matthew and Kyle knew exactly what to do. Hot on my tail with their own wheelbarrows, they doubled over when they saw me, pointing and shrieking with laughter. But only for a few seconds. I guess they weren't sure how I was going to take this indignity. At first I wasn't sure myself, but luckily my sense of humour—or sense of the ridiculous—kicked in and I laughed too. Then, along with one of their friends who had come with them that morning, no doubt just for the cinnamon buns, the boys pulled me up. Yes, it takes three kids to pull one stuck nanny out of a pile of poop. Thank heavens none of my family had their cellphones handy, so Facebook will never see the visual of me losing my poo pile virginity. Guess I became a real farmer that day.

PART II

Within this generation, an extra thirty years have been added to our life expectancy—and these years aren't just a footnote… How do we use this time? How do we live it successfully?

—Jane Fonda, *Life's Third Act*,
TED Conferences 2011

CHAPTER 13

Dear Bill

ON JUNE 2, 2013, I was wakened out of a sound sleep by the stupid chirpy ring tone Matty and Kyle had programmed into my cellphone the day they convinced me I should have cool music when someone phoned me. When we had played with ring tone choices, it had not occurred to me that "Happy Days Are Here Again" would not necessarily be appropriate for all incoming calls.

As I groped for the device on the bedside table I was in a state of confusion, not immediately sure where I was or what was happening. This was not my bed or my house. As the next strains of musical cheer filled the room, my mental fog cleared somewhat. I remembered I was in a hotel room in downtown Vancouver, where I was attending a weekend workshop for volunteer organizers of the upcoming Alzheimer Society of B.C. Walk for Memories event. (currently called The IG Wealth Management Walk for Alzheimers.) Earlier in the year I had volunteered to chair the first annual Abbotsford walk. I had been attending the society's weekly support group for families of people living with Alzheimer's and got enthused by the guest speaker, who captured my imagination by describing the need for an Alzheimer's awareness walk in Abbotsford. Other communities in BC held Walk for Memories events every January, during Alzheimer's Awareness Month. Why couldn't we? *Why couldn't we indeed?*

We could be part of a province-wide fundraiser and awareness-builder. We could rally the community to support the work of the Alzheimer

Society. We could organize a fun event that would produce positive results. Seems my newly retired PR brain was still functioning. I was already writing press releases in my head. Up went my hand. "I'm in," I announced. The walk was just under a year away. We needed to liaise with the BC branch of the Alzheimer Society, form a committee, find a location, seek out community opinion leaders, connect with the major sponsor, set up the entertainment and refreshments, and organize the publicity. My enthusiasm pole-vaulted me into the committee chair position, and I became responsible for overseeing the success of the whole thing.

Six months later, however, my zeal for this project was waning. Bill's health had worsened and my focus had turned inward, away from the community at large and more towards his well-being. His dementia had affected so much of his brain that he could barely speak—a crushing blow for a professional actor whose voice had been a major source of his income and a large part of his sense of self-worth. And his body was so weak now that he was wheelchair bound. I visited him at Bevan almost daily, wishing I could take him back home and just hug him to pieces. But I couldn't. During the previous few weeks he had declined to the stage where he mostly just slept. And here I was, a former PR professional, going through the motions of putting the "show on the road," sleeping in a strange bed and fumbling in the dark to answer the midnight call I had been dreading. There it was. The call display confirmed what I knew was coming. Crap. I didn't want to answer that phone.

"Hello," I said, sitting up on the edge of the bed, my free hand clutching the blanket.

"Is that Pauline Buck?"

"Yes."

"This is Martin Taylor. I'm the night nurse at Bevan Village."

I knew what Martin was going to say. I'd known for five years that this day would come. And for the past few weeks, I knew that the call was imminent. I should not have come to the Alzheimer Society's workshop. I should have stayed home. I should have been there for Bill's last moments in this life. He and I had been there for Bill's dad when he died—his family was into holding their loved one's hand while they were passing away. So where was I for Bill? Not there. Off with strangers. I started to cry even before Martin finished his sentence.

"I'm sorry to tell you that Bill passed away peacefully in his sleep a few minutes ago."

Falling back onto the bed I felt a strange combination of relief, guilt, and an overwhelming sense of déjà vu. After living through the previous five years, knowing this moment for Bill was coming yet not knowing when, the reality was uncannily familiar. It also swept me into my deeper past. When I was between the ages of six and sixteen, my mom and dad and I lived with a threatening cloud constantly looming over our heads—sometimes dark, sometimes not so dark, but always there. When I was six years old, my dad had his first heart attack. For the next ten years, he suffered a number of subsequent attacks, until a fatal one when I was in my mid-teens. In those days, hearts weren't treated like muscles to be strengthened as they are now. In the 1960s, if a heart patient had suggested going for a run, their cardiologist probably would have had their own heart attack from shock at the concept. Heart patients were treated more like semi-invalids. "Don't cut the grass or shovel snow," they were told. "Don't live in a two-storey house—the stairs are dangerous for you—and certainly don't get upset."

Despite my dad's heart condition, life carried on for our family. My parents went to work. I went to school. We went on vacations. My parents had friends over. Life was almost normal—except that it wasn't. The question "When?" was always lurking in the shadows. When my dad did pass away, his death was not a surprise. When the doctor came into the waiting room at Toronto General Hospital where my mom and I sat with Dad's sister and family, we knew. He didn't have to say the words. There was even a macabre sense of relief—our worries were over. The cloud had disappeared. But I was still devastated that my wonderful dad was gone. And tears can still spring up when I'm reminded today of something he said or did. He had a bizarre sense of humour, and sometimes his quick wit pops into my head and I laugh out loud. A couple of years after Dad died, I was happy that my mom met and subsequently married George, a man who was a terrific addition to our family. (My mom sure could pick great husbands.) They were together for twenty-five years. Both are gone now

Lying back on the hotel's bed, I reflected that it was all over for Bill. That bastard dementia—or Alzheimer's disease, or whatever people wanted to call that thieving disease—had won. It had stolen the spirit, the mind, the memory, and the essence of the man I had loved for thirty years. Now it had stolen his body too. He was really gone. There was no more "us." There was just me. And his memory.

The disease took Bill quickly in the end. The final stage spanned just five weeks, following my return from a respite week in Hawaii. While I was away, Bill had developed a rash on his leg and, with Dianne's okay, Bevan had sent him to hospital. The staff at Bevan didn't know what the rash was and wanted it diagnosed in case it was something contagious that could spread to other residents.

For most of May, I knew it wouldn't be long until the end. The first time I visited Bevan after getting back from Maui, I found Bill slumped over in a wheelchair sleeping in the hall. When I woke him up and wiped the drool from his lips, he did not recognize me. I was heartbroken and burst out crying. Unfortunately, the confusion of being transported in an ambulance and poked and prodded by all new people in a strange place had been very hard on Bill. After that hospital trip, he had withdrawn completely into himself. He suddenly became sleepy all the time; he lost interest in participating in any of the activities Bevan offered, just ate and slept, and he stopped responding to anyone or anything around him. Then he gave up eating altogether—and just slept. The care aides could not get any food into him. After two or three bites, he would spit it out. I gave it a try too one lunchtime when I was there, and I think he suspected it was me because I was able to cajole him into eating five or six bites before his teeth clamped shut. After that I had to limit my visits to once or twice a week because it was so upsetting to see him that way. Every time I came home from a visit, I was in tears. With my knowledge, the staff stopped trying to force him to eat and just let him sleep. It was obvious that he was waiting to go. The medical profession describes this stage as a person's brain shutting down and their bodily functions quitting. Bev, my counsellor, said his spirit was leaving his body—slowly, a bit at a time—and he was moving on to the next plane. I liked her description better than the medical one. It was less clinical—not so cold—and it comforted me.

During this time, I was never out of earshot of my cellphone. The care aides and nurses at Bevan were great. They called to let me know how Bill was doing—or even to say that there was no change. Every time I saw the care home's name on my call display I jumped, thinking this was "the call." The night it did come, I had to phone Dianne at two in the morning to come and get me. I had carpooled into Vancouver for the weekend conference and did not want to spend the rest of the night in a strange room. I needed to be home in my own bed. And I needed to have family take care of me. When I saw Dianne walk into the hotel lobby to pick me up, I became a puddle of mush. I thought I was ready for this. I wasn't.

The next ten days were full of activities and planning that were so far from normal, I would sometimes forget why I was doing them. The left side and right side of my brain kept crashing into each other. On the one hand, I was making decisions: meeting to plan the memorial service with Rev. Ed Searcy, the minister who had joined Uhill after Alan Reynolds retired, meeting with the funeral director, visiting the lawyer's office, and going through the endless forms the government insists be filled out (in triplicate, of course) after someone dies. On and on these tasks went. Just arrangements.

On the other hand, I would answer the phone or check my emails and become overwhelmed by the wonderful and loving tributes to Bill that were coming in, and I'd start to cry again. Over and over I was hearing him described as such a kind and gentle man—which was true. I just didn't know everyone else knew it too. Earlier in the year, I had been describing to a friend what it felt like to have a husband living in long-term care. "You know, you're married but you don't exactly have a husband. It's sort of like being a widow without the—" I said, but before I could finish my sentence, which would have ended with the word "body," she said "casseroles." She said I was a widow without the casseroles. A fitting description.

Now I had the casseroles too—two tasty chicken dishes with noodles. But thankfully I had more. I was not alone in that fog of confusion. Family, long-time friends, members of our church, and even some of our new friends from the neighbourhood were walking through that maze with me. Starting with Dianne, who had me home in my own bed by four in the morning, then followed up feeding me, organizing the troops to empty Bill's room, accompanying me to the funeral home, and sorting out the final financial requirements at Bevan. Mike and Matthew dashed over the next day to cut my front lawn, "in case people come to visit."

Elaine, my longest and best friend—notice I didn't say "old" friend—jumped on the first ferry from Gabriola Island to be with me. She helped pull together pictures and other tributes for the memorial service and stood by me when the going got rough. We spent quite a few evenings on the deck, reminiscing about the fun times she and John had had with me and Bill. They were the first friends I'd officially introduced my new boyfriend Bill to some twenty-five years before. It was a sunny Saturday afternoon when Bill and I boarded the ferry at Horseshoe Bay for Nanaimo, en route to John and Elaine's that first visit. Two hours later a blinding snowstorm accosted us as we disembarked. We almost didn't get to the small Gulf Island ferry that travels between Nanaimo and Gabriola, and as we slithered and slid our way along the island's windy narrow roads to John and Elaine's, I think Bill was wishing we had taken a miss on this great introductory event. But the weather gods, and good snow tires, got us through our white-knuckle drive safely, and he was greeted with open arms by Elaine and a welcome bottle of beer from John. An hour later, relieved that we had made it and relaxed from the one or two beers he had consumed, Bill was snoring in the easy chair beside the fireplace. Elaine agreed with me that Bill was a keeper.

* * *

The memorial for Bill at Uhill on Saturday, June 15, was a loving and fun tribute to his life. The service started with a moving commemoration sung a cappella by the congregation's small but mighty group of singers. Heartwarming eulogies followed, including Reverend Searcy's personal sermon, which included his recollections of how Bill helped some of the congregation's readers feel more comfortable at the lectern. Dianne did a great job with her "from the daughter" remembrances, which started with a reminder from the lectern to Matthew that he was to make funny faces at her if she looked like she was going to cry. That didn't work. She cried anyway. And two friends recalled some of their memories of Bill. While we were setting up, Ed Searcy had commented that he had never seen a service with so many pictures of the deceased—many of them professional 8 by 10s that spanned a fifty-year career in theatre. I laughingly said that he'd obviously never buried an actor before. Following the open mic reception downstairs, a gathering made fun by this group of professional comedians and good friends, I was escorted home to a barbecue steak dinner on the back deck with family and special friends. I felt extremely well cared for. With such support, I felt confident that I would get through this loss and settle into a new and calmer time, full of gratitude for Bill's life and what he had brought into mine. I just wasn't sure how.

August 30, 2013

Dear Bill,

It was five years ago today that we drove our cars side by side down Ranch Avenue to our new home and our new life. What a time we had, eh? They say you can't teach an old dog new tricks, but we sure showed them, didn't we? Mud on our boots? Who cares? Septic Tank 101? We're on it. And how about that flimsy mailbox? I wish you were here with me to drink champagne and toast our accomplishments.

It's been a strange three months since you passed away. Even though you weren't living in the house, I knew where you were and that I could see you any time I wanted to. I know you are so much better off now that you aren't living with dementia in a long-term care home. And that makes me feel better for you. I also know that whatever part of heaven you are now in, part of you is still here in the house with me. And that makes me feel OK too. Feel free to hang around for a while longer if you want to. You're probably just making sure I'm alright. And I know I will be—in a while. I still love the farm and think life in Abbotsford is OK. I just hadn't thought about the time that I would be loving this all alone. Anyway, "the best laid plans…," as they say.

I have to go now. Remember Terry, our favourite contractor? He's here, and I have to go check on him. He's repairing the ceiling of the carport from the time during our second summer that I got carried away power washing the outside of the house and decided the carport ceiling could use a wash too. Little did I know the building material that had been used wasn't much more than glorified gyprock, and my water pressure made it sag. Finally this summer it got to me and I'm having it fixed. It would be terrible if it fell in on the cars. Obviously I'm still learning things about serious house maintenance.

Next week would have been your 82nd birthday. I'll write you again then. In the meantime, happy fifth farmer anniversary. Wish you were here.

Love, Me

September 7, 2013

Dear Bill,

You would be 82 today. Another milestone for me to celebrate in a different way. The house won't be full of friends wishing you "many happy returns." But it won't be empty either. The family is coming over for dinner and to sample the cake I made—a zucchini loaf. My first. And right from the garden too. (Finally one that grew!) Then on Tuesday, Kyle's birthday, we're all going to his favourite restaurant for his birthday dinner. Imagine, he's old enough now to have a favourite restaurant, and we will toast the day you two always celebrated together, like we always did.

Right now I'm off with Duchess for a walk. Think we'll head over to Mill Lake Park and walk that really lovely trail. There's a bench I like to sit on and feel close to you. It's where we sat our first time there, shortly after we moved here.

You may not be here in person, but it's still your day and it will be special.

Love, Me

* * *

The first few months after Bill's passing were an interesting time. I began to work through some of the stages of "What now?" and hoped that in another few months, I would have my poop in a group. But realized maybe not. My biggest challenge was motivating myself to do something—anything. Luckily, Duchess loved and needed walking a couple of times a day, and come fall, the horses needed to be brought in every night and let out every morning, so that got me up and dressed at a decent time. But after that the day was a bit of a question mark. I allowed myself to just go with the flow and either do or not do whatever I wanted. Some days I was like the Energizer Bunny with the best batteries. Other times I was just the "cheap imitation."

By early October, I realized I had officially been a widow for four months, although it was hard to think of my current situation as being that new. I'd been living without the original Bill for about five years and had now lived alone in our home for more than a year. So my life was sort of the same, and sort of different. When Bill was living at Bevan, I appreciated the phone calls and visits from friends, inquiring to see how he (and I) were doing. After he died, I was warmed by the many cards and emails that came in, but I wasn't able to read them. Doing so was too upsetting. However, by the fall I found myself reading the messages with gratitude—sometimes laughing, sometimes crying.

About a month after Bill died, I was fussing about his clothes. I didn't want to keep them; seeing them every day in the closet we had shared was really upsetting. But I didn't know what to do with them. So, with the help of Mike and Dianne, I moved Bill's clothes into the spare room closet. There were a few things that Mike wanted to have, so that worked out well. But I was still casting about for an idea as to what to do with Bill's clothes permanently. I knew an idea would come eventually, and that challenge got solved around Christmas.

Back in the 1970s, I had worked as the secretary in the Promotions Department of the *Vancouver Province* newspaper. My favourite task was to type the weekly columns written by humourist Eric Nicol. In this pre-computer age, every Wednesday Eric would bring me the three columns he had written for the next week, and my job was to type them onto yellow copy paper and take them up to Editorial for processing. Being an ardent fan of his, even before I went to work at the paper, I felt privileged to be typing his columns, and exceedingly pleased because I was the first person to enjoy his unique and often hilarious take on life. One day I asked him where he got his ideas from and he said, in a very confidential tone, that once a week a little green man came to the door and dropped ideas through the mail slot.

The winter that Bill's clothes were still in the spare room closet, the little green man came to my door too just as a freezing cold snap hit the Fraser Valley. The idea I had been waiting for arrived in one of the local newspapers—a front-page story, no less. The Salvation Army was looking for volunteers to "man" their Christmas kettles. The article was accompanied by a photo of an Aldergrove couple I knew from my Rotary Club. Sporting Santa hats and Christmas bells, they stood beside a Sally Ann kettle in one of the local malls. My thoughts immediately turned to Bill. He had always been a big supporter of the Salvation Army. At Christmas it was his charity of choice, and we could never pass one of their kettles without him stopping to make a contribution—often quite a generous one. So I thought I might call the number published with the story and volunteer to jingle their bells for a shift or two for Bill.

Then of course the penny dropped. I finally connected the dots. I remembered that the Salvation Army provided warm sweaters, socks, underwear, and so on to people experiencing homelessness and to the working poor in need. The programs also provided quality clothes to men needing something appropriate to wear for job interviews. I phoned the number listed in the paper, managed to ask the questions about the clothes and the kettles without bursting into tears, and made the arrangements. Dianne came over the next day to help me pack up Bill's things. A Salvation Army volunteer came to the house the day after that to pick up the bags. That was really hard—handing over the big green garbage bags full of Bill's clothes. Another milestone. The next week I was booked into Walmart for a two-hour stint of bell ringing, which turned out to be a fun thing to do. People are very generous, and little kids passing by with their parents love to help ring the bells.

* * *

In year one after Bill passed away, facing special days without him often felt strange. That said, the first Christmas without Bill went quite well. There were times during the day that were difficult, when sadness washed over me, but for the most part the day wasn't too bad. I appreciated having Mike's sister, Kris, and Carol and Dan, Mike's mom and her husband, with us. During dinner, their presence helped deflect attention away from the symbolic empty chair at the table. There was a lot of laughter and good times throughout the day, along with some tears as we remembered Christmases past. I couldn't help thinking about the year before, when we had shared Christmas dinner with Bill at Bevan, and at some point we all said how glad we were that we had done that.

In March I celebrated Bill's and my twenty-fifth wedding anniversary with Dianne. The plan was to open a bottle of champagne and watch the wedding video together. The wedding rehearsal, the ceremony, and the reception are all captured on video, but the best part of the "show" is the reception. Many of the guests were comedy actor friends that Bill had worked with for years—a group of fun-loving people who can't help themselves, they have to be funny in a crowd. And they were. Unfortunately, the day Dianne and I had planned to watch it, I couldn't find the video. So instead, we went out for lunch to a great Greek restaurant nearby, ordered a drink, and proceeded to recite the reception, laughing all through lunch as we remembered who had said what. The reception was so memorable that twenty-five years later, we still knew everyone's lines.

Bill's speech to the bridesmaids had brought the house down because it went on and on and on. He thanked every guest who came by name and commented how much the friendship of each was appreciated. In the middle of Bill's speech, Norm Grohmann, one of his *Dr. Bundolo* colleagues, called out, "Let's all raise our glasses of flat champagne!" to which Bill replied, after the laughing died down, "Give me a break. It's my first time"—a dig at Norm for having been married more than once. Dianne decided partway through the speeches that she wanted to say something. She wanted to let everyone know how happy she was for me and how much she liked Bill. Unfortunately, the first words out of her mouth caused an uproar in the room. "Of all the men my mother has known…" At least five minutes of wisecracks and laughing ensued, with *Bundolo* bud Bill Reiter calling out, "Would everybody please turn in their keys?" My heart went out to her as the room's impromptu performers put a temporary end to her heartfelt speech. But she stood her ground and just waited till the pandemonium died down. Then she continued. She really was a trooper to have put up with all those jokes.

Distributing the ashes turned out to be a challenge for me. Bill was not an avid golfer, boater, or mountain climber (perish that thought), so there was not a logical place where I could plausibly offer up his remains in a way that would be meaningful to him and to me. By the spring of 2014, not quite a year after Bill had died, I had selected three locations that I thought were fitting. One was in the water beside my favourite bench at Mill Lake. The other was at the Crane Library on the UBC campus, where Bill had recorded textbooks for use by visually impaired students. Two of Bill's Crane friends were still readers there, and when I called to suggest this, they agreed it was a great idea. They pointed out a spot in the garden just at the back of the library where Bill used to go at break time. Dianne came with me because when she was a student at UBC, she used to go over to Crane to visit Bill and his fellow readers. After I deposited the ashes, we four went over to the Student Union Building for lunch. The third spot was also at UBC, under a tree at the Chapel of the Epiphany where the University Hill Congregation worships and where we had been married. I didn't want to make an event out of distributing the ashes there. I didn't want anyone from the congregation to know it was happening—just Ed, the minister, and me. So one Sunday after church, he and I went together to the spot I had selected, dug around a bit at the tree's roots, and buried some of the ashes there. Ed read a short passage, and we spent a few minutes in silence. This small ceremony was extremely moving. I knew Bill would have liked that spot, and sometimes I go past that tree when I'm out at Uhill and say hi to Bill. The small amount of ashes left over are still in a little container on my dressing table.

With year one of widowhood behind me, there was a feeling of finality that hadn't been there before. I had been living alone in the house for the ten months before Bill died, but it wasn't the same as this. It had felt like living in limbo. Now it was real. Summer was just around the corner—another cycle beginning at the farm. Another cycle beginning for me.

CHAPTER 14

Is there love after death?

I DECIDED THAT I WOULD not send out the thank-you cards that funeral homes provide in their package of bereavement materials. I would wait and send personal notes in Christmas cards to people who had played a special part during all the life changes I had experienced. But there was one friend I wanted to see and thank in person. Don had been a special friend of Bill's since they were in school together, and when I entered the picture, he and his wife had welcomed me warmly into their circle of friends. His wife had passed away seven years before. I knew Don was upset about Bill's death and I wanted to acknowledge his friendship and support with more than just a thank-you card. When word got out that Bill had died, Don was out of town and was not able to get back for the funeral, but sent a heartwarming email.

So towards the end of September, I called Don and arranged to drive in to his apartment in Burnaby to see him. Over coffee we chatted a little about Bill and the memorial service, then our conversation turned to some ordinary "What's new?" topics. Don had enjoyed his vacation, I was thinking of buying a new car, and so on. It was a nice get-together, but our meeting also felt awkward. I thought that was probably because in all the thirty years we'd known each other, we'd never sat down and had a one-on-one conversation alone. There were always other people around—and often a crowd, usually at a party he and his wife were hosting or dinner at our place. After an hour or so I made a move to leave. At the door Don gave me a nice hug and the same little peck on the cheek that I always got when we visited. On the way home I felt pleased that I had made the effort on Bill's behalf to reach out to Don. *That was that.*

Two days later I got an email from Don asking if I would like to have lunch. I was surprised to hear from him and wondered why he wanted to get together, but I accepted his invitation. *Why not? Lunch out would be a nice change.* And it was. For the next two and a half or three months, Don and I continued to get together for lunch probably once a week. He would either drive for an hour to pick me up or we'd meet somewhere between Burnaby and Abbotsford. At first we talked about Bill, then about his late wife and about the general loss of a spouse. It was healing for me to be able to talk so frankly about my feelings to someone who knew Bill so well and who had been through what I was experiencing. We also talked about our triplicate-crazed government and the forms they insist that the newly bereaved must fill out. He laughed when I told him about the run-in I'd had with my bank manager. The bank wanted to cancel my RBC Avion Visa card because I wasn't part of a duo any more—I was a single now. The bank had some sort of senseless policy that failed to acknowledge a twenty-year customer's excellent credit rating. After writing a scathing letter to the president of the Royal Bank, I received word that my Avion card had been reinstated. Ah, yes. I could still wield a mighty pen.

Soon Don and I added some "remember when" conversations to our lunches, reminiscing about the fun we four had had together and with our other friends. I was glad to have this friendship, and I thought Don felt the same way. But the day came when our "just friends" felt suddenly different. Don had invited me to join him at a huge Christmas fair he knew about. Every imaginable piece of indoor and outdoor Christmas decor was for sale there, from lights and ornaments to wreaths of all sizes, inflatable reindeer, and giant Santas. I didn't know at the time that Don was a real fan of Christmas trimmings. Myself, I do the basics and am happy with that. But, since I didn't have anything else to do that day, I decided to join Don at the fair. The plan was to have lunch later. I arrived a few minutes after he did. As I walked through the parking lot towards the front door of the hall, I saw Don standing inside looking out, waiting for me. I smiled and waved. He smiled back. But there seemed to be something different about the way he was looking at me. In an instant I got all jittery. I had a sudden constricted feeling in my chest as if my heart had jumped and took a short intake of air—like a gasp.

The whole time we were at the fair, I felt nervous and uncomfortable. I wasn't interested in buying anything but felt I should so I bought the same stuff Don did, all the while thinking, *He probably thinks I have no imagination of my own.* It was awful. Then at lunch I was tongue-tied (most unlike me) and probably hopelessly boring. I couldn't even decide what to order, and we were in one of my favourite Italian restaurants. *What is happening to me? Why am I feeling so peculiar?* Finally lunch was over and I could scurry home—back to the safety of my familiar barn and fields. I figured Don would never contact me again.

A few days later he did, in an email, his usual form of communication. This was the turning point. He invited me to his apartment for lunch. Not to a restaurant. Or to go shopping. To his apartment. Somehow I knew he didn't have ham sandwiches on his mind. But what was he thinking? What was *I* thinking? It had been a long time since a man had offered to "show me his etchings," as it were. Actually, it had been a really long time since a man had offered to show me anything. I thought about Don's email for a day or two. First I had to make sure in my head that I understood the purpose of the invitation. It seems I did. Then I had to decide if I wanted to accept. I did. I realized the beginnings of desire were blossoming after a lengthy drought. If I thought I was nervous at the Christmas fair, I was a wreck driving in to Burnaby that day and walking into his suite. *Would we be compatible in bed? Would this ruin the warm friendship we had developed? Would this turn into something more? What would Bill think?* Without getting into a lot of details, suffice it to say that two hours after arriving, a very relaxed and happy me was helping to decide where we would go for an early dinner—ham sandwiches having never materialized.

Now what was happening? Was this just a one-night (one day?) stand? Were we an "item"? Was I in some sort of relationship with Bill's best friend? Christmas was just around the corner. Would we do something together? New Year's Eve was almost as close. Would he ask me out? Would he call? Was I sixteen years old all over again? A few days after our first intimate rendezvous, Don and I met at his place for more non-ham sandwiches but made no follow-up arrangements. At that time he plainly said that he would like to keep our friendship just between us. "I'm a very private person," he explained. "Sure," I replied, with stars in my eyes. And, to my peril, I didn't give a thought to what he might have meant. I was too excited about this surprising and wonderful turn of events.

While all this lunching was going on and happy bedding was getting started, life was carrying on as normal at the farm. Horses in. Horses out. Water buckets back and forth to the barn. Snow shovels at the ready. There was no mention from Don of a Christmas get-together in between family commitments, or any plan for New Year's Eve.

After making it through my first official Christmas sans Bill, I found myself getting all anxious about New Year's Eve. I didn't want to spend it alone. I wanted to do something special with Don. Yet I was torn because of Bill. Was this being unfaithful? Yet as each day after Boxing Day came and went, I began to realize that nothing was going to happen. My inbox was sadly silent on the subject of New Year's. And since our relationship was new, if it was indeed a "relationship," I didn't feel I could call Don. Actually, having been out of the dating loop for so long, I didn't know what action was appropriate any more. And were we dating? I didn't know. So I did nothing—just got sadder and sadder.

Then on December 30, Elaine called from Gabriola to see how I was doing. I burst into tears and blubbered my whole sorry situation to her. When the flood finally subsided, she suggested I hop on the next ferry and come over. I think it took me about ten minutes to throw a toothbrush into my bag and head out the door, barely slowing down my car as I dropped off Duchess at Dianne's for boarding. After a quick stop to pick up champagne and some pâté, I was off to the Island. Disappointed as I was that I hadn't heard from Don, I was happy to be going to Elaine and John's. We had a wonderful time—we relaxed, walked in Gabriola's scenic Oceanside Drumbeg Park, talked, sipped champagne, and toasted wonderful friends at midnight on the 31st. I stayed for another couple of days, grateful for being so well cared for. In the meantime, "How was your Christmas?" emails started flashing back and forth on my cellphone between me and Don. I told him I was on Gabriola. Would I like to stop by his place on my way home from the ferry? he asked. Hmm… what a concept. I did my best to stay calm as I accepted his invitation. In my mind, spending a day with him after a wonderful few days with Elaine and John rounded out a perfect beginning to the new year. I was a happy camper, having quickly buried all my hurt feelings about not being invited to spend New Year's Eve with him.

While parts of the first year after Bill died were difficult, I discovered, thanks to Don, that there are more ways to make hay than watching the grass grow long. After we became lovers, we saw a lot of each other. With a bit of a chuckle, we both referred to our new relationship as being "friends with benefits." Sometimes the "friends" part was just the opportunity to get together and talk—time spent that I valued greatly. I felt extremely comfortable talking to Don about Bill and discussing upcoming milestones in my first year without him. Don was also supportive when I needed a shoulder to cry on or just an understanding ear. We even had a conversation about where I should scatter Bill's ashes. We also got into in-depth conversations about world events, politics, and life in general. Don's personality was different from Bill's, and it was fun and interesting to get to know him better. His values were basically the same as Bill's, but he had different opinions. And a wicked sense of humour, which I liked.

Sometimes we got together just for the "benefits." Of course, often we had both benefits and talk. Occasionally, but not often (him being a "very private person"), we went out on what looked like a true date. On Valentine's Day we went to dinner at a terrific Italian place that we both knew well. Then we went to a concert of Rodgers and Hammerstein's romantic music from their Broadway shows. To be honest, the concert was my idea, for Don wasn't keen on going out anywhere other than for a meal. And truth be told, my Valentine's evening was not as romantic as I had hoped. Don was not a hand-holder during the love songs. And at dinner his main topic of conversation was the old days when he and a bunch of his friends used to go to that restaurant a lot.

Generally I benefited from Don's company and found that I was smiling a lot. Soon I felt that I was in love with Don. Looking back now, I realize this relationship was right out of the "rebound playbook." But I didn't see that then. Only later did I understand that what I was really in love with was the idea of being in love—and being part of a couple again. In addition I loved the fantasy that with Don I was going to get my old life back. We would reunite with old friends—pick up where my other life had left off. When I asked "Mr. Private Person" if he had mentioned to his daughter that we were seeing each other, he said he hadn't. "She would tell me I shouldn't be in a relationship with you because you're too vulnerable," he said. I assured him, with a sure sense of self-confidence, that she was wrong. "I'm not vulnerable. I'm okay," I insisted. *Why not?* I was having too good a time to start analyzing my psyche.

Living an hour away from Don was a bit of a challenge, but without either of us saying anything about it, we took turns travelling. He would come out to my place or I'd go in to his. I must have been acting like a sixty-seven-year-old teenager. I told my bridge-partner girlfriends that I was seeing this great guy, and they were all excited for me. Dianne had to know too, because she dog-sat for me when I went into town. Plus, she knew Don from visits to our home in Vancouver and from our wedding. Months passed, and one day, the most hilarious thing happened. It was midafternoon on a midsummer day, and Don was at my place. His Mercedes was in my driveway and his person was in my bed. First the phone rang. I ignored it. Then there was a knock at the door and Duchess started barking. We chose to ignore that too. Finally, I heard voices outside that eventually died down and stopped. By then we were just lying there pretending we weren't home, trying not to laugh.

Turns out my friend Sara, who owned a gardening company called Canada Goose Services and was doing some work in my garden, had dropped by with some plants she thought I would like. Seeing my car in the carport and wondering who owned the snazzy convertible parked beside mine, she phoned. Then knocked. In the meantime, Dianne showed up to take some stuff out to the barn and was accosted by Sara. "Where's your mom? Whose car is that? Why isn't your mom answering?" Dianne, guessing exactly where I was and knowing perfectly well who owned the car, said, "Gee, I don't know. She must be out. She doesn't tell me everything, you know." After Sara finally left, Dianne headed out to the barn, no doubt killing herself laughing. Don and I picked up where we had left off and Duchess went back to sleep. Needless to say, Sara called later to ask what I was up to. And, of course, I told her. I was not the "very private person" in this relationship.

There were problems though. When we first got together, Don said he wanted our relationship to be just between us, that he didn't want a lot of people to know we were seeing each other. He also said that he went to social functions and had lunch with a few other women friends, but assured me those relationships were just platonic. I was okay with that. Plus, since we lived an hour apart, I knew we couldn't just drop in to see each other on the spur of the moment, or call and say, "Why don't you pop over for a drink or dinner?" We were having, in effect, a bit of a long-distance romance.

But we did share a number of mutual friends—couples we had socialized with when Don's wife and Bill were still alive. After we'd been seeing one another a couple of months, I started to wonder why we were always just by ourselves, not meeting up with any other people. I brought up this topic a few times and got the same "very private person" response. Don also said that the friends we all had enjoyed from before were not around any more, that the old get-togethers weren't happening now. I didn't add that we could make new friends. But I sure thought it. He did tell one couple that he was seeing me, but we only got together with them once, when I suggested we go out to a play and then dinner. I also wondered why I was never invited to dinners or gatherings with his family, all of whom I knew from the past. Our relationship was starting to bother me. I wanted more. He didn't. And I started to feel that there must be something wrong with me. *Why is he keeping me away from anybody else?*

Every February, good friends of mine and Bill's organized the most delicious roast pork dinner in their home. Don, a true-blue carnivore, loved roast pork and knew this couple too, so he accepted the invitation I initiated for him to join the group. I felt absolutely wonderful walking into their living room with Don and introducing him to those he didn't know. I loved having him as my date. He was friendly and joined in the conversations, some being comedic banter that he contributed to with the best of them. And the food, as usual, was terrific. But I'm not sure whether Don had a good time. On the way home, he asked, "Was that okay?" Looking back on the dinner, I think he felt self-conscious, but I never figured out why. And he never suggested we get together with those folks again.

Around mid-April, Don and I split up for a short time. Trying once again to get him involved with other people, I suggested he join me at Dianne and Mike's house for a dinner of Dianne's fabulous ribs. I thought this was a great idea. After all, he knew Dianne, and this evening shouldn't pose any sort of threat to whatever it was that kept him at arm's length from others. My invitation to him was by email, like most of our communications, and he emailed back saying that the dinner sounded lovely but he didn't want to come if he would be made to feel he was being presented as "'Mom's new boyfriend." This comment launched a few emails between us, during which I complained again that we never saw other people and he said I just didn't get it that he didn't want to be in a "boyfriend/girlfriend" situation. So, in a flurry of keystrokes, we chose to stop seeing each other.

In shock, I emailed him back and said that if he wanted to break up with me, he had to at least do it on the phone or in person. An email split was too modern for me. He said he was busy at the moment but would come out to the house in a week or so and we would talk. He did come out and we had a long conversation. He said he understood that I was hoping he would be like a boyfriend, but that he couldn't make that kind of commitment. He said he didn't want to hurt me, but also he couldn't change. This was not a new conversation. We had had it quite a few times before. Don had always broached the subject, asking me if I was sure I was still okay seeing him and saying he felt bad that he couldn't give me the relationship I wanted. And I always lied, saying I was happy with our arrangement. You know, half a loaf and all that. The one thing we also always said and agreed on totally was that if either of us met someone else we wanted to be with (in the Biblical sense, that is), we just had to tell the other, and we would part great friends. The inference here was that someday I would meet someone who could or would make the kind of commitment I needed and Don would be happy for me.

So, still thinking I was in love with Don, and having spent the past couple of weeks really missing him, I said I could live with that. And we got back together. For the most part we remained the lone duo, only visiting back and forth, but one time he invited me to spend a weekend with him in Seattle. He had two tickets to a theatre production. Would I like to come? *Would I?* I jumped at the invite. And we had a great time—we ate well, played well, did some shopping, and enjoyed the show. It didn't occur to me to think it was a bit odd that he already had two tickets to that show before asking me to join him. Who buys two tickets on spec? However, at the time, I was still imagining signs that his resolve to remain hermit-like was receding.

Because I was still commuting to the west side of Vancouver to attend church services at Uhill, I sometimes saw Don for lunch after church or I'd do a Saturday-night sleepover, then go to church from his place Sunday morning. If it sounds a bit strange to spend the night with your lover and then pop off to church the next morning, I can only say it felt a bit strange too. But there are some things in life I just leave up to God to deal with. Unfortunately though, seeing Don continued to upset me. His ongoing insistence that we not socialize with other people made me feel like I wasn't good enough to share a conventional relationship with. He kept insisting the reason wasn't me; it was him. And of course, I kept trying to change him.

One Sunday in October, after we'd been seeing each other for a year, I gave up trying. It was the week after Thanksgiving. I had met him in a restaurant near his place after church. All through the meal he had regaled me with stories about the great time he and his family and extended family members had had at their Thanksgiving dinner. The more he told me, the more I felt like crying. Midway through my soup, I escaped into the women's washroom to get myself under control. I felt so left out and unwanted. When lunch was over and we were preparing to leave, he said, "I'll give you a call later in the week," which is what he always said. I blurted out, "No. Don't. I don't want to see you any more. I love you so much and it hurts too much to hear you talking about what a great time you had but you won't include me. Please don't call me anymore."

As I said this I felt absolutely crushed, but at the same time relieved. How much longer could I beat my head against this wall? Don said he was sorry that he couldn't give me what I wanted, then added that he might wake up tomorrow and realize what a mistake he'd made. Ever the smart-mouth, I quipped, "Well, if you do, you know where to find me." I then got up and went out to my car, where I sat and cried before pulling myself together for the drive home. Needless to say, if he did feel sorry the next day, he resisted the urge to call. And, tears notwithstanding, I knew I had done the right thing. I knew he wasn't the right fit for me. But boy, it hurt to say goodbye.

Ode to a Broken Heart

Have you ever had a new pair of shoes that seemed absolutely perfect? When the clerk opened the box for you to try them on, you were instantly excited. They were sophisticated in a way that was so subtle it gave the appearance of being somewhat casual in the right light—the perfect shoe for any occasion. When you slipped them on, you felt like a million bucks. They complemented your legs and made whatever you were wearing look like a page from a fashion magazine. Their reflection in the mirror made you smile. How fast could you get your Visa card out of your wallet? When you got them home, they were given a place of honour on the shoe rack in your closet, and every time you knew you were going to be wearing them, you got excited all over again.

But it wasn't long before you noticed the tiniest little sensitive spot on one baby toe. Each step came with a very minor twinge. Never mind. It was really nothing. And it was worth it to show off the new shoes in public. When strangers saw them, they smiled. You and the shoes looked so good together. After a while, though, a little red mark appeared on that toe. Even when you were just shuffling around the house in slippers, your foot still felt uncomfortable; nothing huge, just something wasn't quite right. A little Band-Aid helped for a while. So did massaging a drop of oil on the inside of the shoe where it rubbed, to stretch it out a touch. But eventually it became obvious that the new shoes did not fit, no matter what you tried.

Have you ever wished you had your old shoes back again? They weren't quite as sophisticated as these ones and their excitement had diminished somewhat over time, but for the most part they were comfortable and you felt good wearing them. Strangers nodded approval at those shoes too, and friends really liked them. Occasionally they pinched a bit, but nothing that couldn't be smoothed out.

The problem was, the old shoes were gone. And the new ones couldn't be worn any more. They hurt too much. You had to make the ultimate decision to stop wearing them. So you pushed them to the back of the closet, where you couldn't be reminded on a daily basis how much you still loved them. Over time the sore spot on your toe started to heal, and you congratulated yourself on making the right decision. But once in a while something jostled one of the new shoes to the front of the closet and you were reminded how great you felt wearing them. They still looked fabulous. But sadly, looks aren't everything.

Have you ever had a new pair of shoes like those? Me too.

* * *

That fall, I also stopped going in to church at Uhill. For one thing, driving for an hour to worship was a bit over-the-top, especially considering that Trinity Memorial United Church, which had an exceptionally good minister, was about ten minutes from my home. But more than the distance, I realized I was going to the Chapel of the Epiphany for a number of wrong reasons. I loved the services at Uhill—great minister, moving music, wonderful and supportive friends. But, I'm embarrassed to say, I had started to link the chapel to visits with Don, which was so wrong. And to my life with Bill. We had been married there and were active in the congregation. Even though I didn't sit where we had always sat, I was always reminded of our life there. So with a view to exorcising all my ghosts, I bade my friends at Uhill farewell and joined Trinity United in Abbotsford.

In the six months following that fateful breakup with Don the Sunday after Thanksgiving, I sunk into bouts of sadness and depression that seemed insurmountable. I had trouble sleeping. My heart was breaking and I cried alone in my bed most nights, never having felt so lonely in my entire life. Some nights I woke up having a panic attack, wondering if this was what a heart attack felt like. I suddenly had nothing. My husband of twenty-five years was gone, along with the great life we had had together before his illness. And now his friend, my hope for new happiness, was gone too.

My life had no purpose—and I had no reason to get out of bed. My professional career was over. My job as a full-time caregiver was finished, and widowhood doesn't come with instructions. I didn't know what to do. After Bill died, I never experienced the heart-wrenching loss of him that I expected new widowhood would bring. That was probably because the true essence of Bill had been gone for so long before he passed away. I had been mourning his loss a bit at a time, experiencing what I learned to call "anticipatory grief." Then, when the time came that I should have been adjusting to my new situation and contemplating my future options on my own, Don had burst on the scene, filling the gap. I had now dropped into a confusing period of grief, not sure whose loss I was crying about: Bill's or Don's. Looking back at that time, I see that I was mourning the loss of both of them, but that I had them mixed up in my head.

My stepfather George had a funny T-shirt that said, "I may not be perfect, but parts of me are excellent." Parts of both Bill and Don were excellent, and I started to realize that I had been trying to shake both men up in a Mason jar and pour the best of each into one ideal package, without any of the parts that weren't perfect. And there were some of those. For example, Bill snored. He also had some habits that were a tad obsessive and annoying. Like, it took him five minutes to get out the door when we were going out. He had to check and sometimes recheck that the stove was turned off, or that the alarm was turned on. And Don could be a bit of a know-it-all at times and seemed to need to one-up others in various situations. I also saw that with Don, instead of moving on, I was trying to return to the past. Unfortunately, the old life I was looking for didn't exist anymore. The former socializing crowd was gone—friends had moved away, passed away, or just lost interest. In other words, the dream life of my memory could not be recreated. Don had kept telling me that, and I had not accepted it.

One night, sitting up to my neck in bubbles in the tub, a location that was fast becoming my go-to spot for deep thinking, I had an epiphany. By trying to recapture the old Vancouver life from Abbotsford, it dawned on me that I would never move forward. I couldn't keep trying to recreate Don in the image of a Bill that I wanted back. I also realized that not only had I lost my husband, I had also recently lost a good friend, someone who had played a major role in our life for over thirty years and in my personal life for almost two. So, leaving a trail of bubbles on the bathroom floor, I threw on my housecoat and dashed down the hall to my computer. Strike while the iron is hot and all that jazz. I wanted to see Don. To explain where I had been coming from and that I didn't want to throw away our friendship. Capitalizing on our old "friends with benefits" theme, I sent him an email with the subject line "Friends *without* benefits," hoping he would respond. He did, and we arranged to meet for dinner in Langley.

It was a great evening. I told him that I realized why I had been trying to change him. He told me he was sorry I had been going through such a bad time. He also had the good grace to say he was sorry he couldn't change. We laughed some, I cried some (I do that), and we left agreeing to be friends without benefits. I felt really good.

It didn't last, of course—the "without benefits" part. There was obviously some sort of chemistry between us. The physical attraction still drew us together. The whole relationship was pretty much on its last legs though. For about the next year we visited back and forth, but there was little sense of togetherness and we had minimal involvement in each other's lives. I was always glad to see him though. I did still enjoy his company, but I had (finally) quit hoping that our get-togethers would be anything more than an enjoyable diversion. Yes, just sex—with my eyes wide open. Everyone deserves just pure pleasure sometimes.

CHAPTER 15

I can do this (sort of)

THERE WAS ALWAYS A LIST of things that needed doing in the yard and garden, and if they didn't get done before a three-or-four-day spell of rain, the weeds would outgrow the carrots and the front lawn would start to make the house look like it had been abandoned. Balancing the weather-dependent needs of the outdoor projects with my frequent desire to do something else, such as relaxing in the house with a book or going out for lunch, was challenging. One particular day in early fall though, I was determined to catch up on all the outside projects. The forecast was calling for warm, bright sun until early evening, when a storm front was scheduled to roll in. *Perfect.* To-do list in hand, I hit the ground running.

First I pruned my tomato plants and directed them up the new metal stakes I had bought from Lee Valley, that amazing purveyor of tools, gifts, and creative solutions for household and garden needs. Next, before Matthew rode over on his dad's lawn mower, I headed to the front yard to trim around the trees with my brand-new battery-powered weed whacker. I was so excited. Up until that day, I had been borrowing Mike's gas-powered weed trimmer, but he always had to get it going for me. As you know by now, I'm not mechanically inclined, and any machine with moving parts is not my friend. When Mike fired up the trimmer, the process looked so simple: press the primer bulb, move the choke lever, squeeze the throttle, yank on the pull rope, and the weed whacker roars into service. For me—not so much. After five fruitless pulls, dead silence. Start over. Move the choke lever, squeeze the throttle, jerk the pull rope six or seven more times. Still silence. When the #@!% machine still doesn't start, stamp your foot and yell rude words at it. More silence and an almost dislocated shoulder. The logical solution? Buy a battery-powered weed whacker and simplify your life. No moving parts. Just charge the battery, slip it on, and presto! Look out, weeds. Here I come. Well, almost presto…

When I bought what I thought was going to be a boon to this non-mechanically inclined farmer wannabe, a highly organized friend advised me to store the battery on the charger so it was always ready when I was. Good strategy. I brought the new garden toy home, set up the charger, and snapped the battery onto it. *Brilliant!* Smiling with glee, I envisioned my new anxiety-saving device (ha ha) slicing through those offending weeds like a hot knife through butter. Problem was, on this planned day of accomplishment, a.k.a. lesson one in *Weed Whacking for Dummies*, I couldn't figure out how to get the battery off the charger and back onto the machine. Where's the Release button I'm supposed to push? Not *more* weed whacker frustration! Thank heavens Mike was just down the street and always cheerfully stopped what he was doing to help me. "Just push here," he told me. "Thanks." Next the shaft needed adjusting so it would actually whack the weeds, not thin air. Was that in the directions pamphlet? Not that I could see. So back to Mike's for that lesson. "Just push here, then twist," he said. "Thanks so much." The final straw? The nylon cord that actually cuts down the weeds was missing, and I needed to replace it. Even with my frustration level over the top, I managed to figure out for myself how to attach the new cord. (Fortunately, I had a roll of cord from my "adventures" with Mike's machine.) By this time I was feeling too embarrassed to show up on Mike's doorstep yet again.

After releasing most of my pent-up aggravation by assaulting the long grasses that the lawn mower could not reach, I turned my attention to a patch of overgrown grapevines. These were blanketing the side of the garden shed and had been bugging me for most of the summer. After an hour of attacking these vines, my blood pressure was back to normal and that section of the yard looked much tidier. In the meantime Matthew had arrived, cut the lawn, and left. Kyle, who was within calling distance, then came to help me drag the giant pile of grape leaves that I had whacked down to the compost pile.

Next to my favourite new yard implements: snap-on hose fixtures. I spent a happy half-hour rearranging the hoses and sprinklers to make watering more efficient. In addition to being challenged by weed whackers, I'd always had a tough time screwing and unscrewing all the hose attachments and extensions I needed for watering the front and back flower and vegetable gardens. It might be a left-handed thing, I don't know, but I've never been able to screw items together easily. I always seem to be turning the parts in the wrong direction. Well, no more. John and Elaine on Gabriola Island had shown me their connectors that just snap the sprinklers and hoses together for ease of rearranging and extending the watering system. I could not get home fast enough to buy some for myself. John also put me on to those new hoses that start small and "grow" when the water is turned on, just like *As Seen on TV*—lightweight, easy to move around the yard, and compact to store. Thanks to these new fixtures and my electric weed whacker, things were definitely looking up in the yard-maintenance department.

After I'd attended to a couple of other small projects, it was almost five o'clock and the sky was starting to change. I could feel the gorgeous day slipping away. Time to quickly finish off the chores: check the barn to make sure there was enough food for the chickens, and collect the daily eggs. With serious-looking rain on the way, I moved Sassy into the middle field to give her access to the shelter. In the summer, she grazed down the long grass in the front field, but because of the way the fences and gates were arranged, she couldn't get to the barn on her own from there. And she hated getting soaked.

Finally, time to go inside, pour a glass of wine, and pat myself on the back for a day of great accomplishment that included overcoming some of my deficiencies. Heading up the back stairs, hoping for a chance to relax on the deck before the rain made its appearance, and thinking how well I was keeping the place going on my own, I heard, rather than saw, unnatural movement behind me. Turning, I was horrified to spot fifty chickens running wild all over the backyard, and Duchess, first on the scene, having a blast chasing her new playmates. The gate to the hens' yard had sprung open and they had made a dash for it. The next few minutes were like a scene from a Keystone Cops movie. The chickens were tearing around in circles. Duchess was barking and rushing everywhere. And I was zigzagging back and forth, trying to grab the dog to put her in the house while simultaneously trying to shoo the chickens back into their pen, all while debating whether to stop and call the kids down the street for help. I decided not to call, figuring that by the time they arrived, either all the chickens would have had a heart attack and died (they have weak hearts that can do them in if they're startled), and Duchess would be contentedly picking feathers out of her teeth, or I would have succeeded in rounding them up. Success reigned supreme—almost: no more chickens in the yard that I could see; no more dog going crazy. Another disaster averted.

Back on the deck, medicinal-size glass of wine in hand, I was shocked when Duchess made another Olympic-style dash down the back steps and across the yard. Glancing up, I heard that ghastly sound llamas make when they're riled up (this is when you stay clear of their spitting end). What I saw was a chicken trying out for the one-hundred-yard sprint through the horse paddock. I'm afraid the expletives that flew out of my mouth were considerably more than I would have wanted the neighbours to hear and definitely more than Mike's uncooperative weed whacker had had to put up with. But I was really pissed. What next?

Down the stairs I flew, out to the back field, absolutely furious that this was happening, and also feeling totally sorry for myself. After such a busy and successful day, why couldn't I just sit and relax on the deck peacefully, celebrating my achievements? While creeping around outside the barn, doing my best cheerful "Here, chickee" call, inside I was agonizing. *If I lived in a condo, I wouldn't have to do all this. I could spend my evenings—and my days even—just relaxing. Why do I have to deal with all this chicken chasing crap?* Given another minute or two, I could have added many more items to the list of injustices I was tallying, including a wad of poop on my shoe picked up from beside the poo pile. But believe it or not, that wonderful pony Cassidy saved the day. When he saw me standing in the shelter catching my breath, he came running in from the field, looking so glad to see me that my heart melted. I knew he was just after any treats I might have in my pocket, but that didn't matter. He was so cute, and when he rushed up to me it felt like he was saying, "It's okay. I love you."

As for the rogue chicken, I gave up my search—never did find her. I suspected she was safely hiding in tall grass somewhere and would probably appear the next day. Or maybe not. Some things on a farm don't need to be dwelled upon. Back on the deck again, refreshed wineglass in hand, I thought once more about how none of this could happen if I lived in a condo. But how many condos come with loving ponies you can hug?

* * *

By the time year two of being Widow Buck rolled around, money worries had joined my lengthy list of farm challenges. Everyone said that after a spouse dies, the remaining partner shouldn't do anything rash or make any life-changing decisions for at least a year, especially about selling the house and moving. After Bill died, I had no plans to move. I really liked the house and thought I could probably handle the work that the farm needed. After all, it wasn't as if the property was a real working farm with cows that needed milking at 6:00 a.m. And the family was still down the street, available to help.

Initially Bill and I had been doing well financially. Thanks to deposits to our bank account from Bill's RRIF, rent from the tenants in the basement suite, and the old age security cheques we both received, we had been in good shape. But when Bill moved into Bevan, the household lost the use of his government pensions. That money went towards his long-term care. At first I didn't notice the reduction in my spending ability—things just ticked over by themselves and I was fine. But eventually this loss of income started to catch up with me, mostly because of increased home maintenance and repairs. Condos in the city may not have adorable llamas to visit, or economical farm status at tax time, but they also don't have expensive septic system repairs or chicken coops generating winter hydro bills high enough to heat Buckingham Palace. I realized I needed to either get a job (now there was a ghastly thought) or figure out how the farm could earn its keep.

With some guidance from Dianne, it was agreed that one solution would be to put the barn to work. The plan was that I would rent out the stalls, boarding other people's horses for money. To make room, we would move Sassy and Cassidy back to Dianne's place, their original home. Dianne said renting out the stalls was called "self-board." The horses' owners would provide all the food and come over every day to clean the stalls. (Thus I wouldn't have to stoop to poop shovelling. I still had my limits.) My primary job would be to let the horses in and out, as I had been doing with Sassy and Cassidy, and throw them their breakfast hay. I visualized I would probably also check on such things as fly masks and blankets as the needs arose and spoil the boarders with treats, one of my favourite things to do. I really liked being around horses.

But even though I wanted a self-board arrangement for people needing a place to keep their horses, I was cautious about who to rent to. Because of the daily presence of the horse owners on my property, I needed to make sure I rented to reliable people. The solution was found. My first boarder was Amelia, the daughter of Dianne and Mike's friends. Amelia was the young girl who had come to our first Thanksgiving bonfire a few years back, and spent the entire evening mooning over Sassy and Cassidy at the fence while the rest of us roasted hot dogs and ate s'mores. She was now sixteen and had been pining for a horse of her own for quite some time, but at her place there was no barn. It was perfect that I knew her parents too, partly from a bit of socializing with them at Mike and Dianne's and mostly through their younger son, who spent lots of time playing in our hayloft with Kyle and Matthew.

Amelia's first horse was purchased, a stunning ten-year-old quarter horse named Lady who was fully broke, gentle, and had a great disposition. When Amelia's parents transported Lady to my barn and gave me my first $200 cheque, I was thrilled. Amelia came daily, grooming and bonding with Lady, and soon started saddling her up for beginner rides in the paddock. Most days her mom and dad came too, and within the first few weeks, Lady was visited by one set of grandparents, two aunts and uncles, Amelia's brother, and, of course, her best girlfriend, to whom she was joined at the hip—teenage girls, you know. I expected it wouldn't be long before the family hitched up the horse trailer and progressed to riding the horse trails in the area. I loved seeing such a happy kid enjoying her new horse so much. Because Lady was the only boarder, Cassidy stayed on in my barn to keep Lady company, while Sassy was back at Dianne's, bossing around the other horses that lived there.

In the good weather, Lady was outside 24/7 along with Cassidy and the two llamas. Come winter, I would be letting the horses in and out morning and night, as usual. What I hadn't realized was that the fall and winter in-and-out routine would be more challenging because of Lady. Being reasonably wise to the ways of horses by then, I knew that Lady would need a bit of coaching to get from the field to her stall. The new evening routine of being called in would be foreign to her. So, for the first couple of nights, Dianne, Amelia, and I showed Lady the ropes, opening the barn's side door and calling. With Cassidy leading the way, it took only a couple of days before Lady came dashing across the field and trotting into her stall like a long-time resident. Seems a bucket of horse treats situated in the far corner of their space can turn any steed into a quick learner. Turns out, though, that getting some help in the mornings would have been good too.

On the first morning, after I opened the barn door and then the stall door, Lady just stood there and stared at me. "What am I supposed to do now?" was written all over her face. Remember, I was used to Sassy automatically heading out. My first solution was to let Cassidy demonstrate how the morning routine worked, so I opened his stall door, fully expecting him to head right out. Big mistake. He thought being let out was his invitation to rush into Lady's stall. Now I had to contend with the two of them in one stall. Lady, who wasn't up for visiting, dashed into the middle of the barn, but instead of heading out the door, she circled the shed row in search of a treat bucket. I'm not afraid of horses, but when you are standing in a confined space with two tons of animal mass that has a mind of its own, you tend to be cautious. And when that animal mass isn't sure what it's doing, or where it's supposed to go, you stay very ready to quickstep out of the way.

Fortunately, at that moment, Cassidy got with the program and trotted out the barn door. Lady followed. The next morning I was a touch wiser and reverted to all parents' fallback strategy—bribe psychology. Open the barn door. Open the door to Lady's stall. Move towards the barn door while simultaneously shaking a bucket of horse treats. Then stand aside as she zooms by, grabbing a mouthful of goodies on the way. Ta-dah! Success.

My other financial hope for the farm was that the vegetable garden would yield enough produce to be a viable weekend business at the local farmers' market. But after six years I was still not into gardening, be it vegetables or flowers. I loved to eat the produce and admire the landscaping that Sara, my professional gardener friend, had created along the back fence. But I just couldn't work up any enthusiasm for digging around in the dirt myself, even though I made the effort every spring and summer.

Yes, some veggies made it and they were delicious

It occurred to me that agricultural students from the University of the Fraser Valley might be looking for some land to start a productive vegetable patch. It seemed sad that so much of my property was just going to waste. The students could learn how to grow produce in clay soil, of which I had an abundance, and the harvest could go to food banks and farmers' markets. For free use of my space, I would share the produce with them. (Or maybe they would share it with me—not sure which.) Unfortunately, nobody was interested, which was too bad. I still think it was a good idea. So I finally gave up on the pipe dream of a lucrative garden. That any produce at all matured and became edible was primarily thanks to Sara, who had done the planting and popped by to make sure my occasional bouts of weeding were adequate.

I did find work outside the home though. In the last few years of Bill's working life, he had joined the group of actors who worked as extras on film and TV productions. They formed the crowds or were the pedestrians walking back and forth across the street behind the action. When we lived in Vancouver, if Bill's agent advised that a production needed more extras than there were professional actors available, I occasionally took the day off work and went along with him. I found the work fun and was appropriately star-struck the day we were involved in a production with Jack Nicholson. Since the Vancouver film industry was on a roll, I now decided to go this route on my own. I got an agent, had photos taken, and when I was called, headed off to set. The plan was to augment my income and to make some new friends in a different environment. With all the people involved on a shoot, I thought I might strike up a friendship and possibly even a new relationship with a person of the male persuasion. Even though Don was still on the scene, our relationship was showing no signs of developing into anything deeper.

As it turned out, the life of an extra—or "background person," as they prefer to be called—was not for me. The hours were terrible, the working conditions were often uncomfortable, the money was only okay, and everyone I met while sitting around in the tent waiting to be called was more interested in bragging about their last gig than becoming friends. Boring. So I gave up my foray into the film industry. Maybe one more self-board in the barn would do the trick.

CHAPTER 16

The bloom is off the rose

In the summer of 2015, almost seven years after Bill and I had pulled into the driveway of our new life, it was time for me to back away—alone. I had become overwhelmed by the amount of upkeep that the farm needed. I was also experiencing emotional problems that included extreme loneliness, anger, and boredom. Friday morning was Rotary. Tuesday afternoon was bridge. And occasionally there was lunch or a get-together with Don. Other than that, I was alone on the farm with practically no outside stimulation in my life. Evenings were particularly difficult. There was nothing to look forward to when the day's work was done—nobody to sit with on the deck enjoying the beautiful sunsets or to curl up with in front of a romantic fireplace. And it was really a drag that Don was so far away. Had we been living closer, and had our relationship been a bit more traditional, I imagined we would naturally pop back and forth evenings as couples do.

The decision to leave had not come lightly, and it had not come without many mixed emotions. Part of me knew I would look back on my farm days with indelible memories: "Don't you hate it when your balaclava steams up your glasses?" I used to say to Bill. "Can you believe I crawled under the belly of a racehorse to attach a winter blanket?" I bragged to my friends. "Okay—a former racehorse, but hey, that's still huge, right? And what about that poo pile, eh?" And I knew I'd look back and remember Bill too—the new life and adventures we made for ourselves during his illness, a life I would not have missed for anything. The other part of me found it tough to know I wouldn't be seeing my almost-teenage grandsons as often. I had loved watching out my living-room window as they rode their bikes back and forth on the street after school. And I'd welcomed them with joy when they dashed through my front door and out the back on their way to the hayloft, to continue the games they had started the day before. But I knew that it was time to move on—to leave Mrs. Farmer Buck behind.

For about a year before I finally decided to put my gum boots on eBay, I was faced with one unforeseen repair and rebuild problem after another, all of which were beyond my ability to handle alone. In addition to the usual lawn, garden, and barn demands, high winds knocked down the fences—not once, but twice in one week; the stream that intersected the back field was overflowing from weeks of non-stop rain and needed dredging; and the backyard required a major fix. It had become so bumpy to walk on that the risk of a broken ankle loomed large in my mind. I was told by Gerry next door that a previous owner had laid down peat moss to use the backyard as a riding ring. Then a subsequent owner had covered the peat with soil and grass seed to make a traditional lawn, but over time the peat had started to sink, leaving a backyard that was lumpier than a pan full of tasteless Christmas gravy. It was like the newbie farmer gods had conspired to test me. "Is she really farmer material or should we send her back to condo land?"

On the surface, the solution to each of these situations was simple: phone the family. But I was loath to do that. I knew how busy they were with their own lives: Mike had a full-time job, their farm needed attention on weekends too, their preteen boys were actively involved in extracurricular activities, and Dianne's dog-breeding business was taking off. I felt guilty when I called them for help, and cranky that I had to.

In addition, relations between me and Dianne had become strained, which contributed to my reluctance to ask, yet again, for help. Dianne had been totally there for me all through the first year after Bill's death and before, when he was in long-term care. But during the second summer after Bill died we drew apart—then over time, we actually came apart. I'm sure my loneliness added to the bad situation. And my anger. I was mad all the time. Mad that I was alone. That there was no one to talk to or to share the easy chores with: trimming the bushes, weeding the garden, or collecting the eggs. And there was no one to sit with at the end of a busy day, to applaud our good work or admire the beautiful sunset over the back fields. After Bill died I had expected year one without him to be difficult, with all the firsts to get through: Christmas, birthdays, wedding anniversary, and so on. Interestingly enough, those firsts were not as bad as I had anticipated. Family and friends rallied around to lend support. And I guess it helped that I was expecting these difficult occasions, so was sort of mentally prepared.

My serious upset didn't really start until year two—the year I wasn't mentally prepared for. By then, everyone else's life had gone back to normal, to what they had been doing before. Mine had not. Living just down the street from the family, I could see their friends coming and going for drinks or dinners and I wished they were inviting me to come too—especially since I knew many of them. I wouldn't necessarily have joined them every time, but it would have been nice to be asked. It felt the same as when Don didn't invite me to join any of his family gatherings, or refused to socialize with any of our mutual friends. I was feeling totally deserted and rejected on every front. Not to mention completely sorry for myself. Was there something wrong with me? It seemed to me that the family didn't care. They didn't see how lonely I was; how I would kill for an invitation to their house, for dinner or even for afternoon coffee, or a five o'clock glass of wine. When I mentioned, as casually as I could muster, that it would be nice to come over to their place for dinner some night, Dianne's response was, "We practically never have a scheduled dinner hour anymore. We're so busy." I couldn't understand why they didn't get it—didn't understand that I wasn't just asking for a meal. I was asking for emotional support. I was really hurt that I had to ask and even more so that I was being refused.

Being dependent on Dianne and Mike for farm work was also becoming a problem for me. I hated it that I had to ask for help every time I couldn't do something myself. And when Mike or Dianne came, I felt it was more from a sense of duty than love. We talked about this once and came up with the plan that I would give them a list of what I needed doing and they would fit it in with the to-do list at their place. The idea was good in theory but in my mind it didn't work. Giving them my list made me feel totally inadequate. When I finally asked Mike and Dianne if they had any ideas how the backyard lawn could be smoothed out, they primarily shrugged their shoulders and said they didn't know. Maybe they'd just had enough of the needy mother down the street.

So, feeling somewhat like the Little Red Hen who couldn't get any help, I attacked the problem myself. I got a quote from a landscape gardener to rip up the whole backyard, bring in a few truckfuls of good soil, and plant new grass. I would have a gorgeous lawn of putting green quality—all for a mere $5,000. Needless to say, that was not an option. Instead, I arranged for delivery of a load of topsoil to fill in the many grooves and low spots, enlisted the help of a neighbour with a backhoe to distribute the dirt, and rented a heavy roller to flatten the lawn. The plan was to then seed the yard and wait for a much-improved, more level and safer lawn to grow.

The appointed day for this work dawned hot and sunny, with temperatures that ultimately climbed up to 28 degrees Celsius (well into the 80s). By the time I had driven to the rental yard to get the roller, which weighed a ton I'm sure, and darn near killed me as I was getting it in and out of my trunk, I was in a major snit—hot, cranky, and mad that nobody in the family had offered to help. Worse than that, during all this backyard action, Dianne and Mike, along with one of their friends, had come over to clean out the llama's pen behind the barn. *They are right there. Doing nothing for me.* I was even more furious. Another neighbour had pitched in by "lending" me the teenager who worked for him on weekends, a delightful kid who provided much-needed muscle power, taking turns with me to heave the heavy roller around the yard. But it was when I had rolled dirt over the third or fourth major groove on the lawn, sweat pouring down my face, that I decided to sell the farm. I didn't need all that aggravation. Take me back to condo living.

The next day, I did call a realtor but decided not to list the farm at this time. I felt I was too much of an emotional basket case to make such a huge decision. But I knew condo land was looming in my not-too-distant future. Even though there was much I still liked about the farm, I could see that the time was coming for me to make some major changes in my living arrangements. I was also starting to realize that I could never move on with my life or figure out who I could become on my own if all my energy was focused on trying to handle all the never-ending farm work.

As for the lawn, by day's end, it was smoother but covered in dirt. The next morning, before I had purchased any grass seed, Mike came over and offered to arrange with a provincial highways workman he knew to sell me some of that green hydroseeding material that maintenance crews spray on mounds of dirt during road construction. It seeds itself and turns into grass. I appreciated Mike's offer and thought his idea was a good one, which it was. Soon the backyard looked decent and was reasonably safe to walk on—not as smooth as a putting green, but hugely improved.

Next came what I now call "nasty November." It was probably the most challenging and, quite frankly, most expensive month I'd experienced in the six years I'd been on the farm. First came the monsoon rains—days and days of rain that turned into what seemed like weeks and weeks. To help keep us all sane, every few days the clouds would disappear and the sun would come out, giving me a chance to wade around the property looking for problems. Fortunately, neither the house nor the barn ever flooded. But because of our high water table, all the fields were covered by "Buck Lake," which became a swimming hole for the ducks and geese heading south. That part was a bonus—for them. And fun to watch for me. The horses, however, were totally underwhelmed every morning when they saw they had to splash out to the back forty to find some dry land. One good thing was that when the rain stopped, the ground absorbed the water fairly quickly.

The real water problem was the stream that flowed (or didn't) through the property. It ran north-south along the east side of the fields and formed part of a series of small waterways that crossed a number of the farms in the area. My portion came from the property across the street via a culvert under the road. Unfortunately, during heavy rains, the stream tended to back up and overflow. Since moving to the property, we had been fortunate that every couple of years, Gerry's son had offered to dredge the stream for us. Coming over on his days off with his giant Cat, he had scooped out the grasses and sediment. That year, though, he had a job out of town and was not available, so I hired the services of another neighbour who was a heavy equipment operator. What a monster machine that Cat was up close. And what a great job it did. After just a few scoops of sludge, the water started to flow again and the backed-up water dropped substantially. My neighbour across the street was glad too, because when "my" stream backed up, his did too. The other great part of hiring the Cat was that preteen Matthew and Kyle were allowed to sit up in the cab and work the digger's controls. They absolutely loved it. And yes, Mike had a go at it too—must be a guy thing,

But feeling like we had survived the remake of the movie *Noah*, we were then hit with days and nights of below-zero temperatures and 70 kilometre per hour winds. Quick—hook up the water heater and find the warm coats and balaclava. Even Duchess was in favour of exchanging her morning constitutional for a quick pee and fast dash back to the fireplace. My morning reconnaissance tours started at 7:00 a.m. just outside the kitchen door, where I rescued and tied down whatever had flown around the upper deck overnight. Next came the property perimeter check, looking for downed fences and gates. Thank goodness the horse fences survived, but not the fence that divided the backyard from the middle field. On day two of the windstorms, I discovered one of the six- by eight-foot cedar panels had been separated from the fence and was lying unceremoniously on a pile of horse poop in the adjacent field. That looked familiar. Didn't I have that fence problem last winter? Sigh…

Borrow Mike's pickup truck. Head off to the lumber yard to buy a replacement section. Call for help to install the new fence panel. Four mornings later: Repeat. Yup, another cedar fence panel had not survived the night. Was there no end to this? The forecast was calling for more rain and wind starting immediately. I hoped the fence would stay up this time. But if it didn't, my plan was to buy another lottery ticket, hope it won, then spend the cash on something more exciting than new cedar fencing. *An all-inclusive vacation in Mexico would be nice.*

Without me knowing it, Dianne and Mike were as upset as I was about our strained relations around this time. "We were really worried about you and didn't know what to do about your rage," Dianne told me the day we sat down together over beer and wings at the local pub to clear the air. "We didn't really come over to work on the llama pen the day you were fixing your lawn," she explained. "We came to keep an eye on you. We didn't know how to help but we wanted to be close by." Hearing Dianne say that she and Mike were worried made me feel better.

I said that I didn't like to keep asking them for help. I felt guilty that I was bugging them. It was after my second beer and probably sixth barbecue wing that I dropped the news I was planning to move.

"I don't want to go far," I said. "I'd like to find a sharp looking and affordable townhouse somewhere nearby and watch the hired landscapers handle all the outside work." We laughed about that and I think Dianne understood where I was coming from.

> **FOR SALE**: One 3,000-square-foot split-level house with (illegal) income-generating basement suite on a five-acre farm. The property includes a somewhat winterized barn, fully operational chicken coop (chickens not included), mismatched cedar fencing between slightly lumpy backyard and horses' fields (horses not included), fully functioning hayfield, somewhat overgrown vegetable garden, and recently dredged stream.

Yes, it was time to trade in the bales of hay for a tiny patch of townhouse grass with flowering shrubs in a pot and a vegetable store down the street. But I planned that my new place would be close by. I could still nuke a mean bowl of popcorn and entice the boys to come over. I wasn't sure what my next chapter would look like, and I really didn't care just then. I simply knew it was time to close this one out. In spite of all my newly developed rural skills, I couldn't keep playing Farmer Buck forever.

For the first ten days or so after the realtor's sign went up in February 2015, there was a flurry of activity around the listing—practically a showing per day, and some days two. Then activity slowed down for about a week, before picking up again. Apparently rural properties don't have open houses like places in the city—or they didn't then anyway. Realtors made appointments and brought their clients in one at a time. Also, unlike city listings, rural properties do not sell overnight. It took time for just the right buyer to come along. I noticed that potential purchasers were as interested in the fields as they were in the house. These were "real" farmers who were coming by. They needed to know what crops would work here. Fortunately, I wasn't in a hurry to sell, but keeping the place spotless all the time wore a little thin. And I discovered the perils of over-vacuuming the carpet; I swear my poor living-room rug became threadbare.

All the "how to sell your house" manuals say you should remove everything personal from all the rooms and totally clear off the kitchen and bathroom counters. Do they think prospective buyers don't clean their teeth? Or make toast? Nevertheless, I faithfully swooped through those crucial rooms before each showing, stashing the implements of real life in drawers and cupboards. And then, when the looky-loos had left, I couldn't find anything. After the realtor's first showing, it took me one whole day to relocate my kettle. I was just about to ask Rose next door to invite me for coffee when I remembered I had stuck the kettle on the top shelf of the linen closet. I had tried to jam it into the oven, but that space was already taken. I just hoped the potential new owner didn't open my broom closet and wonder why the knife holder and cookie jar were sitting on the floor beside the Swiffer mop. I expected they'd understand though, because perhaps they were going through the same thing at their place.

I didn't know where I'd be moving to, but as I said, I definitely planned to stay in the area. The whole idea of moving to Abbotsford from Vancouver had been to be near the family, so there was no sense moving too far afield. My hope was to find a well-appointed townhouse with a nice view and easy access to enjoyable walks for Duchess. In the meantime, while I looked forward to a return to condo living, I enjoyed my last spring as Farmer Buck. Since I was looking for a townhouse, not an apartment, I guess the term should more accurately be "strata living." For some reason, "condominium" is only used to refer to apartments. But any condo is still a situation with maintenance taken care of by a council of owners.

When the farm sold in the spring, I stipulated a fairly long closing date, so I didn't feel rushed into finding my new home. As it happens, I found it quite by accident on Mother's Day weekend in 2015. Two or three friends had told me to go see an elegant-looking gated community of townhomes they knew of that included landscaped walking paths and water features with streams and fountains. In addition, the complex allowed dogs, which was a bonus. My search for accommodation so far had revealed a definite lack of dog-loving strata councils, especially if the dog was a full-size poodle.

That year Mike's mom, Carol, came down from Summerland for the Mother's Day weekend. On Sunday, she and I took Matthew and Kyle to a salmon release event organized by the Abbotsford Ravine Park Salmon Enhancement Society. Families went to a local salmon habitat stream and were given buckets of salmon fry to pour into the water. Most of the fry had been raised at the hatchery, and some at local elementary schools as part of the environmental educational program. The boys loved this activity and went back for more and more buckets to release into the wild. When we were done, I noticed that we were just a few blocks away from the address I'd been given for that townhouse complex my friends had recommended, so we drove up the hill to see it.

Well, it was love at first sight for all of us. Since it was a gated community, we couldn't get in to the grounds, but we could stand with our noses pressed up against the wrought-iron gate and admire the look of the place. The thirty-acre complex included 159 townhomes nestled in a parklike green belt that featured forested walking trails and a natural creek. As we peered in, a woman with a full-grown golden retriever on a leash walked past. Dogs! Perfect! The boys weren't happy that I was leaving "their" street, but when I told them this place had a clubhouse with a pool, they decided pretty quickly that it was okay for me to move, so long as it was to there. Later they were even more enthused about Nanny's new place when they heard about the 50-inch TV that was going into my new family room downstairs.

From this...

To this

It's fun to look back at the image I had made to announce the move from our Vancouver condo to the Abbotsford hobby farm. I remember grinning to myself as I put that card together. Our city friends had been razzing us about becoming stars of the new *Green Acres*, the popular 1960s sitcom. And I must admit I enjoyed the fantasy of being mistaken, on paper at least, for Eva Gabor. I even got a Photoshop-savvy friend to paste our faces onto the *Green Acres* poster for the front of my card. I thought Bill looked much more handsome than Eddie Albert did in the original photo, and I looked rather good wearing Eva's body—who wouldn't? The new moving announcement card, however, just showed a picturesque fountain peacefully gurgling within the townhouse complex.

A few realtor and lawyer appointments later, I found myself in the last stages of buying my new home, a pretty two-level, three-bedroom townhouse with almost as many square feet as the house I was moving from. Hooray—no downsizing for me. While still in decision-making mode, I discovered that the pool in the clubhouse offered aqua fit classes three times a week—definitely another selling feature. Maybe I could yet get an Eva look-alike body of my own.

After all the property transfer documents were duly signed and initialed and my deposit cheque was delivered, a wave of nostalgia washed over me. I guess that was to be expected. The farm had seen me (and Bill) through thick and thin, and now after seven years I was leaving it. But I knew leaving was the right thing to do, and I knew I'd feel better soon. I loved my new home and was keen to go, but it was hard to walk away from a place that was so full of life-changing memories: being part of the boys' progression from preschoolers to young teenagers; watching my daughter grow her dog-breeding business while managing the day-to-day demands of their farm; and, of course, experiencing the ups and downs of my own life. I still can't pass a display of zucchini in the grocery store without ruing my gardening failures. (Sometimes friends send me pictures of zucchini plants they grew that are so large it takes two hands to hold them. I laughingly think that's mean of them.)

Before the dismantling and packing started, I needed to walk through the place and quietly remember our life in each room, saying goodbye and thank you for the hilarious highs and heart-breaking lows that were life on the farm. I remembered that first morning when I had picked my way around the boxes and clutter everywhere, having no idea what lay ahead but excited about the adventure. Then there was the banging and crashing as the contractors converted the 1970s kitchen and bathrooms into photo-op candidates for *Better Homes and Gardens*; the languishing with Bill in the giant soaker tub, up to our ears in bubbles with no legs hanging out the side; the many evenings we'd sat quietly on the deck with a glass of wine, admiring the graceful beauty of the horses as they grazed in the back field. Then there was the time we had to reassure a concerned neighbour that all was well as the fire truck roared up, after Bill set off the alarm by burning the kettle on the stove. I recalled welcoming friends for barbecues and tours of the barn that included offering treats to the llamas. And finally there was the day I stood at the front door watching the ambulance take Bill away to the hospital. That was sad.

* * *

Even though the new townhouse was large, I did need to do some pretty serious sorting and purging before the move. Bill and I had leaned a bit towards packrat syndrome. We weren't the horrible hoarders you see on TV, but we did tend to hang onto things… you know, just in case. And it was time to get rid of a lot of it, which was hard for me. I found that some of the stuff I was getting sentimental about wasn't even mine—or ours. It was boxes of things Bill had been lugging around from place to place for years, including his dad's tools—drills and saws that we never used. Hell, that we didn't even know *how* to use. And photos from his family's basement of people I didn't know. Plus records, CDs, out-of-date sound systems, and the usual household detritus that accumulates. Lucky for me, I had some great packing and sorting help, including from Arlene, my regular housekeeper, who spent one whole day efficiently filling and labelling boxes. Dianne came over to help as well.

When Mike's mom, Carol, heard that I had bought into the complex we had all admired, she said she would visit again and help me organize a garage sale. She was a regular volunteer at the Summerland Health Care Auxiliary Thrift Shop and was a whiz at pricing and displaying. The day before the sale she was in her element, setting out tables, pricing and sorting things, and giving me lots of good advice, not the least of which was identifying what things needed to go straight to the dump. "Do not pass Go and do not collect $200." Just take it away before the sale.

Ever the PR type, I decided to make the garage sale a fundraiser for the Rotary Club's Starfish Backpack Program, a project the club had implemented in Aldergrove that provided food for hungry schoolkids on weekends. I figured the charity aspect would increase attendance at the sale, thereby moving out more of my stuff while also supporting Starfish. And it worked. At the end of the day, there wasn't much left in the carport, and Starfish was over $800 richer.

The sale would not have been quite as successful if Mike had not been there to help with the electronics. He set up one of the sound systems to give us music during the sale, then proceeded to sell it out from under us to somebody who came by. Oh well. Who needed music anyway? Later a guy who had seen the garage sale ad phoned for details about something electronic—a woofer or tweeter? Mike took the call, talked that mysterious technical language to him, and ultimately sold that system when the prospective purchaser showed up. Then there was Dianne, the money person, who was in charge of the cash box. The boys primarily added to the ambience of the day, offering visitors goodies from the cookie jar and generally just being helpful. Carol was great at talking up the visitors, and a couple of Rotary Club members also came to help out. By the end of the day, we all fell into the remaining lawn chairs, beers in hand, pooped and happy.

Not to be forgotten, arrangements were made for the residents of the barn. Lady went to Amelia's place, where her dad was building a stall beside their garage. Cassidy was ceremoniously walked back to his previous home in the family's barn, and the chickens—well, the chickens were treated to a brand new coop and roosts down the street. Mike had built an addition onto their barn for the hens.

I was on my way. But not totally gone. I would still be heading back to the old neighbourhood regularly to get eggs. There was absolutely no way I would be eating store-bought—and I still don't. But before the moving truck had even finished unloading at the townhouse, my first sleepover party was under way, followed immediately by a family road trip. Matty and Kyle had followed the movers in and that night slept on a pile of quilts in the family room. The next day, after shutting the door on a maze of cardboard boxes, we three piled into my car for the five-hour trip to Summerland. Billed as the First Annual Boys' Road Trip to Grandma

Carol's, this trip was a week-long vacation we had planned long before my moving day was set. Because Carol and her hubby didn't live nearby, they didn't get to see their grandsons as often as I did—or get to know them. This trip, without their parents, was a big hit for us all, and was repeated twice more before Matthew and Kyle each got summer jobs. And so it was official: Farmer Buck had officially become Condo Nanny.

CHAPTER 17

Back to condo land

New home. New beginnings

When you are shopping for a new home, you mostly pay attention to the interior. Will my furniture fit? How many bedrooms are there? Does the kitchen need renovating? And in a townhouse complex, is there adequate visitor parking and do the strata council minutes from previous years indicate that the place is well run? What you *don't* usually think about are the neighbours. A cursory glance around the neighbourhood for an overabundance of parked Harley-Davidsons and a quick listen for loud music blaring from windows is about the extent of any environmental research most people do. The rest is the luck of the draw.

At my new place, my draw was extremely lucky. My neighbours were super. (They still are.) The units in this complex don't run in one long row, with a main road through the middle and garage doors cheek by jowl all the way along. The homes are situated in either circular cul-de-sacs surrounded by trees and water features or short rows of just a few side-by-side garage doors. My townhouse is in an area with eight other homes. When I moved in, three of my immediate neighbours were widows like me in various stages of adjustment. I befriended them easily and we got together fairly often, especially in the summer, to share appies and a glass of wine on one of our sundecks. We also ran back and forth a bit the rest of the year—somebody always needed a cup of sugar. One of the women had remarried, which was great because her new husband was very handy. He took it upon himself to help fix things for all of us, and in payment, we kept him plied with good red wine.

This couple has since moved, but the new neighbours are equally as congenial. The woman who lives immediately next door to me has become a good friend. We have each other's keys for house-monitoring during vacations and for emergencies, and we walk each other's dog if either of us is going to be late getting home. We also bake a mean Christmas cake together.

There are many advantages to living in a strata situation. For one, somebody else cuts the grass. I tell my friends that my favourite day is Wednesday because that's when the landscapers come. The snow is shovelled by an outside service, and I found that living in a gated complex creates a feeling of security. But living in community also comes with rules: no double parking in front of your garage, no leaving Christmas decorations up past January 31, no multicoloured window coverings, and any awnings installed on the decks must be a colour I love to call Strata Beige. Even though I was an experienced condo dweller from a previous life, and fully understood the need for guidelines, after seven years of absolute freedom on a rural five-acre property, the transition back to condo life took a bit of getting used to.

In my case, the adjustment centred around Duchess. No more could I just open the back door and send her out to do her business anywhere she wanted to. There were rules. Dogs must be on a leash. Results from their "business trips" must be picked up and deposited in one's own trash bin. No more flicking Duchess's "business" into the roadside ditch with a stall fork. And excessive barking was frowned upon. While all of these rules made perfect sense, my main concern was how to stay dry while walking the dog in the rain. With a bit of creative thinking I figured out the answer, and within the dog-walking bylaw too. I came up with a practical plan that worked beautifully—with one minor flaw. In addition to wanting to stay dry, my other concern was not scaring my new neighbours on rainy days when I took Duchess out wearing my farm garb. I also knew that at 7:00 a.m., I wouldn't want to take the time to get all decked out in my official keep-dry ensemble.

Well, it looked like I could still stay dry for the first outing of the day. Right in front of my entrance and next to my garage door was a small section of grass. On her first trip to her new home, Duchess chose that spot for her emergency trips in between real walks. So on our first rainy day, my plan was to open the garage door, stand under the overhang to keep dry, and let her dash out and dash back. If this is sounding a bit familiar, you have me pegged. What I hadn't counted on the first time I tried this was the black Lab that lived down the way. He was being walked past my place at the exact moment my garage door came up. Being surprised by the sudden movement and sound, he jumped and Duchess lunged out towards him, the call of nature completely forgotten. I was instantly in the street too, decked out in my lime green rain boots and my black raincoat, with my pink nightgown dangling loosely underneath. Grabbing Duchess by the collar to prevent an undesirable altercation, I thought I was doomed. So much for good neighbour relations. Was this the beginning of "Who's the crazy new lady in the complex?" The Lab's owner was a man I had chatted to before, while wearing more civilized attire. With a bit of a smile (or was it a smirk?), he calmly said, "A real wet one today, isn't it?" and carried on. *Phew!* Future rainy morning calls of nature included the leash—a long one that still enabled me to huddle under the overhang. And, since I didn't get a note from the strata council to the contrary, my wild green boots got to stay.

* * *

After I was all moved in and settled, Don came over to visit. Helping christen my new outdoor furniture on the back deck, he admired my scenic view of nearby trees and gardens with mountains in the distance and commented that my new home was "very me." I thought so too. I was pleased that most of my furniture suited my new place. A minor change of wall colour in the living room and the purchase of a new area rug created a look that was both sophisticated and comfortable. While he was visiting, Don offered to get me a new indoor-outdoor carpet for my deck as a housewarming gift. That was perfect—just what I needed.

It's fun to brag about being organized. And I am, for the most part. But sometimes my plans go off the rails—literally. Don was bringing the new carpet over in a day or two. In preparation, I moved all the deck furniture out of the way and rolled up the old rug to take it to the dump. A simple plan: all I had to do was carry the old carpet I'd brought from the farm's upper deck through the house, through the garage, and into my trunk. Here's where everything went downhill. After carrying my armful of carpet to the back of the car, I realized I needed swinging room to get the load into the already opened trunk. But the car was too close to the electric garage door and there was no room to manoeuvre. I needed to open the garage. With my arms still full of carpet, I skirted various bits of garage clutter and poked the wall switch with my one available finger. Instead of opening all the way, the garage door stopped partway up. The safety cord that connects to the electric track in the ceiling got caught on the car's open trunk lid and detached the movable lever, converting the garage door to manual operation, a necessary feature during a power failure. No problem. I just had to manually push up the door, put the carpet in, and close the trunk. To reconnect the electric lever, "just yank on the cord again," my realtor had told me the day I viewed the townhouse. "The lever will connect itself to the track and the garage door will once more be powered." Sounded simple. But not for me. I'm sure if you Googled "mechanically inept person," my picture would pop up.

When I pulled on the cord again, nothing happened. Staying calm, I backed the car out of the garage, got out the handy-dandy stepladder that the previous owners had left, and climbed up to see what moved, caught, or changed when I pulled on the cord. Nothing was happening that I could figure out. For the next five minutes I was up and down the ladder and over to the wall switch to see if my reefing on the cord had made a difference. Nothing. Finally, in true neighbourly fashion, I called on my friend next door. In the past she had mentioned that her late husband had been very mechanically inclined, unlike mine, so I thought maybe he might have shown her how the opener worked. No such luck. She didn't know either. But she was very willing to help—or at least to join me in my angst. We girls stick together, you know. For the next few minutes, we ran back and forth between her garage and mine to see if we could find a clue about where or how the lever should connect. Again, no luck.

So there we were, standing on the road in front of our garages looking quite helpless, when, lo and behold, who should drive by in his older model Jeep Isuzu Trooper, but Sean, the complex's handyman, Well, I guess it might have been quite a while since he got such a welcoming reception. We both leaped out in front of his vehicle as it zoomed towards us, waved, gesticulated towards my garage, and entreated him to stop. Laughing at us he came into the garage, jiggled my cord (hmm, that sounds a bit racy), and pushed the button on the wall. At first nothing happened for him either. The lever didn't catch but the track's mechanism went back and forth without moving the garage door. Suddenly the lever caught and everything was fine. Turns out the trick is to hold down the power button on the wall long enough for the lever on the track to go all the way to the end. Then it engages with the pull rope, and the garage door starts moving. Who knew? Big thank-yous to Sean and my next-door neighbour for coming to my aid. And hooray for Don, as the deck's new carpet looked fabulous.

* * *

The year was 2017. It had been almost ten years since I'd moved with Bill to the farm in Abbotsford, four years since Bill had passed away, and two since I'd reverted to being Condo Nanny. Oh yes, and five years since I had officially become a senior, although I didn't feel like one. I knew it had happened though because one day the federal government started sending me cheques—*how very nice of them*. The provincial government got into the act too and sent me a shiny new gold-coloured CareCard to replace my other ordinary-looking one, and when I flashed it at the ticket window of BC Ferries mid-week, my trip to Vancouver Island was free—not for my car, just for me. But every little bit helps. And of course, good old Cineplex Odeon had offered me admission to their shows at a reduced rate when I turned sixty-five. I didn't tell them I'd been sneaking into the show as a senior for years. I'd just followed right behind the good-looking grey-haired guy I lived with when he asked for two seniors' tickets. Sneaking into movies seems to be a habit for me. When I was twelve years old, I was doing it in reverse: sneaking into movies that were rated for age fourteen and up. Despite all these acknowledgements that I was sliding towards decrepitude though, I was still up for a party, no matter the excuse.

A seventieth birthday party? You bet. To celebrate the January day that marked the start of my eighth decade on earth, Dianne organized a get-together at my place. The party started with the arrival of Matthew to take down my Christmas tree, a task I couldn't do myself. A couple of weeks before Christmas I had slipped on the ice while out walking Duchess and broken my left elbow, a feat that required surgery and saw me sporting a less-then-fashionable black sling that impeded all movement of my left arm. There wasn't much pain—just a lot of inconvenience for this southpaw. Trying to fish the Cheerios out of my morning cereal bowl with my right hand was truly a challenge. I couldn't do much for myself, including any kitchen work on Christmas Day, so everybody else had to do all the prep. There's a bright side to everything, right? By mid-January, however, I had regained much of the mobility in that arm, just not all the strength. For the birthday party, friends and neighbours from the complex came over for afternoon wine and cheese and admired how competently I held my wine glass in the wrong hand, a parlour trick I had perfected over the previous weeks. Then for dinner, the family and long-time family friend Doug prepared a delicious stuffed roast pork feast with all the trimmings. They did everything, including the dishes, and I felt well cared for and quite spoiled.

While turning seventy didn't made me feel older, other than the occasional arthritic ouch in my index finger, it did cause me to consider where I was at—and where I wanted to be for the rest of my life. In my grandmother's day, seventy was old. Today, more than not being old, seventy can be the beginning of a whole new life, a life that Jane Fonda, in a TED talk presentation to a group of women in 2011, called the "third act." Her premise was that the last thirty years of our life are our second adult lifespan—a new developmental stage during which we can reimagine how we want to live. Of course, we may not make it another thirty years—or our money may not make it (yikes)—but I thought Fonda offered a positive way to step into the future.

Without consciously realizing it, for the previous couple of years I had been laying the groundwork for my own third act: selling the farm, moving to the townhouse, meeting new friends, and increasing my community volunteer involvement. But despite making these substantial changes and keeping busy, I occasionally felt less like Jane Fonda and more like Peggy Lee when she sang "Is That All There Is?" Amidst all this activity there seemed to be an emptiness in my life that needed to be filled. As I've mentioned before, my birthday is my personal New Year—a new age, a time to reflect on my life. Especially when it's one of those Big Zero birthdays. Seventy was no exception. Having set the stage for my next phase, or "third act," as it were, I needed to get on with it. After all, I wouldn't be seventy forever.

As it turned out, I wouldn't be Don's whatever-I-was-to-him forever either. The day after my birthday, I had written a blog post about turning seventy and how good things were for me, except that I missed sharing my life with a loving partner and wished I were in that kind of relationship. The day after that, a little more than three years after our first fateful non-ham sandwich at his apartment, Don called "us" off. I opened my inbox and found an email from him saying that after reading my birthday message, he felt guilty that he couldn't give me what was missing in my life and decided it would be best for both of us if we stopped seeing each other. *There he goes again, breaking up by email.* I, at least, had called it quits with him face to face that day after Thanksgiving.

Instead of being upset, I was mad. We had already arranged to get together two days after my birthday. He was to come out for dinner in a super restaurant we wanted to try, then come back to my place for the night. I wished he had waited till we were face to face to have this breakup conversation. We had said right from the beginning that if one of us wanted to stop seeing the other, we would say so and still be friends. But after reading his email, I couldn't imagine remaining friends. I was really tired of his "I feel so guilty" routine. I figured he probably had someone else in tow—someone who lived closer, some other new widow whom he could dazzle with his gestures of comfort.

If he'd handled our breakup with some class, we could have recovered the long-time friendship that had existed when there were still the four of us. I phoned him, of course, and we talked, but in the end we were no more. We hadn't seen each other in over a month anyway, what with weeks of knee-deep snow, bouts of cold and flu, the Christmas holidays, and my broken elbow. In addition, during all these December challenges, a good friend of ours had passed away and I wasn't even able to get into Vancouver for the celebration of life. I was snowed in.

Yet part of me was glad we were over. I think subconsciously, or maybe consciously, I had forced the situation by writing that blog post. After all, you can only beat your head against the wall for so long before either common sense kicks in or you go through life with an unbearable headache. For me, the headache was gone. All that time I had spent thinking there must be something wrong with me. And it was him who had the problem.

CHAPTER 18

And for my third act...

THAT ANONYMOUS GROUP OF PEOPLE known as "they"—the folks who advise widows not to sell the house too soon, and who also say that keeping busy is a good tonic for loneliness—don't realize that some people with Type A personalities, such as myself, could tend to get a little carried away in the "keep busy" department. To say that I spent the next year going slightly overboard in my attempts to follow Jane Fonda's advice to reimagine my life would be a gross understatement. With no Don to plan assignations with, I found myself jumping from project to project, meeting new people and getting involved in a series of different communications activities. This community involvement was fulfilling, but eventually it became too much.

My whirlwind year started in January 2017, right after my elbow healed. I got the idea to pitch an essay to CBC Radio's *Sunday Edition* with Michael Enright about the day Bill didn't recognize me. I thought telling my story would be a good way to help the Alzheimer Society get its messages out about how the various forms of dementia can impact other members of the family. The story was something I had written previously for my blog, and it appears as the Prologue of this book. CBC liked the story and said they would air it sometime in the year. After I made the few changes to the text that their documentary editor recommended, CBC arranged for me to voice the piece in its Vancouver studio. I had had experience on radio in the past, but never anything like this long-distance taping session. Wearing the "cans," as headphones are called, was new to me. And being directed from afar was also a first. As I read my story into my mic, the Toronto editor I had been working with was whispering advice into my ears from her mic more than two thousand miles away. "Speak slower, remember to breathe, don't shuffle your papers (the mic picks up the noise), and let's take it again from page 2." I felt like a real pro. My piece didn't run until September, but the whole process did wonders for my sense of well-being, and when friends called to say they had heard my story and loved it, I felt great.

Partway through that year, other opportunities to put my PR experience to work started to present themselves. For the Rotary Club of Aldergrove, I organized a media event to publicize the tremendous support the club had received for the Starfish Backpack Program. One sponsor was the Air Line Pilots Association and the pilots who fly for Jazz Airlines, a regional partner of Air Canada. Its Jazz Pilots for Kids program, which organized fundraisers for children's programs, had chosen to support Starfish. The media event worked out well. We got a great story in the paper and on social media, and I felt like I was back in the groove—especially when the pilots' spokesperson, looking fabulously photogenic in his captain's uniform, flew his private plane to the event from his base on Vancouver Island. My self-appointed job was to meet him at the Abbotsford airport and drive him to the celebration of the Starfish program's expansion into another school, an expansion that would not have been possible without the Jazz pilots' funding.

Next, I volunteered to join the Volunteer Cancer Drivers Society, an organization that takes cancer patients to their medical appointments at no cost to the patients. When VCDS board member George Garrett, a retired radio reporter that I had worked with in the past, described to our Rotary club one morning the service their volunteers provide, it occurred to me that I had the time to do that and it would be a good way for me to feel useful. Three months later, I was invited to sit on the society's board as director of communications.

Then I was asked to work with Bard in the Valley, a community theatre company that presents Shakespearean plays every summer in Langley. Working with this organization was right up my alley because two of my former clients had been community theatre groups: Theatre

Under the Stars, a production company that presented Broadway musicals every summer in Vancouver's Stanley Park and The Royal City Musical Theatre Society, which was based in New Westminster, BC. In December 2017, at the Rotary Club of Aldergrove's annual general meeting, I was nominated to the position of president-nominee, which meant that I would be president of our club for the fiscal year July 1, 2019, to June 30, 2020. It also meant that for the next eighteen months, I would be involved in numerous activities and training sessions in preparation for my presidency.

Ten months into this frenetic year of "pick me, pick me," I realized that sitting on three volunteer boards, participating at relevant committee meetings, attending weekly Rotary gatherings, playing bridge regularly, and trying to train a new puppy was a prescription for some sort of breakdown. Ah yes, the puppy. Charlie was an adorable black goldendoodle, an offspring from Dianne's breeding business. Duchess was in poodle heaven by then and I found I missed having a dog. A canine friend was great company and good for my health—their needs got me out of bed; their antics kept me smiling.

Charlie notwithstanding, I had thought that scheduling community involvements Monday to Friday, sometimes 9:00 a.m. to mid-evening, would feed my need for companionship or relationship, or even provide the opportunity to meet someone special. Wrong. Being constantly on the go fed my ego some, but mostly stressed me out. So, with the wisdom of any intelligent woman of my vintage, I cut out two boards, decided to focus my volunteer energy on the work of Rotary, and registered Charlie in puppy training classes. I also established a relationship with a new clinical counsellor, since Bev, my previous counsellor, had retired. Having an unbiased sounding board to talk to about what's important—or what seems important at the moment—can be helpful.

Christmas 2017 was peaceful and uneventful, a lovely and stress-free time with the family enjoying our traditional tree festivities and daylong feasting. And the New Year's weekend was perfect—a welcome turning point. After spending the past few years worrying about what I would do for New Year's and with whom, I was prepared to just go with the flow, not knowing that the "flow" would be so great. Early in the fall, one of my bridge partners asked if I would like to join her, her husband, and their daughter, also one of my friends, at Harrison Hot Springs Resort for the New Year's weekend. They had booked two of the resort's holiday packages, which included two rooms, dinner in the Copper Room, brunch the next morning, and wine sent up to the room. I was delighted to be included in their plans. What with dashing through snowdrifts to and from the steaming outdoor pools, basking in the luxury of a facial and massage in the spa, and dining on perfectly prepared rack of lamb, the weekend was a delightful way to ring in the start to my "revised" third act.

I am glad to contribute what I can to the community volunteer organizations I support, and I enjoy spending time with my neighbours and family. I don't see Matthew and Kyle much anymore. Teenage boys are way too busy to eat popcorn with their grandmothers. But they taught me how to text so we keep in touch the modern way now. And as soon as I perfect my selfie skills, I can show them that I still look (almost) the same. Maybe in my future I'll meet someone I can love as much as I loved Bill. Or get into a relationship not quite as tumultuous as the one with Don—or maybe not. I'm not devoting a lot of time to worrying about it. I'm too excited to see what's waiting for me around the corner. And when it comes, whatever it is, I'm sure I'll wing it just fine.

EPILOGUE

THREE YEARS AFTER MORPHING INTO Condo Nanny, I occasionally get startled out of a deep sleep by a howling wind roaring through the trees just across from my back deck or the pounding of rain on my patio furniture. Sometimes when this happens, my stomach muscles seize up and the worry synapses in my brain hit overdrive as they start running through the possible fallout from this storm: *Will the new fence panels hold overnight? Did I shut the little door on the chickens' coop? Will Sassy and Cassidy give me the evil eye in the morning when they discover Buck Lake is back?* Then, a nanosecond after consciousness becomes reality, I realize I'm not on the farm anymore. The only harm this storm could cause would be to flatten the petunias that grace the entrance to my townhouse.

But, rolling over and snuggling down under my warm comforter, sleep eludes me. Memories in the darkest hour of the night stir up worrisome questions. Did I do the right thing? Should we have moved from Vancouver? What would life have been like if we'd stayed? How would Bill have been if we hadn't moved to the farm? Did I do him any favours? Or myself? What would I be doing now? What *am* I doing now? With my eyes squeezed shut, I know deep within me that moving to the farm was the right thing to do. It gave me the proximity to caregiving help that I needed from family and provided a few fun and unique years in an exceptional environment. But still more questions niggle. Did I do things right? Did I look after Bill the best way possible? Did I handle family relations well? How's my third act going so far? What could I have done differently?

Everybody told me what a great job I was doing. They noticed how caring I was with Bill, and how loving. (Except when I lost my patience, of course, but they didn't see those times.) I know I *was* caring—and loving. But now, in the midnight reflections that still arise periodically, I see there are things I regret. The biggie, in my mind, was that I never initiated a conversation with Bill about dementia. We never talked about how he felt when he heard the diagnosis. What did this mean to him? Did he understand what the doctor had said, what the ramifications were of a dementia diagnosis? I was afraid to ask. Oh, there was the occasional reference to his disease. Like that day at the gas station when he couldn't remember how to put air in the tire. I thought I was reassuring him by saying it wasn't his fault that he couldn't remember. When he said, "Then whose fault is it?" we just hugged.

Then there was that rainy morning I came in from walking Duchess, dressed all in black, and finished Bill's sentence for him when he couldn't describe the eerie sight I'd created coming down the street. I chimed in that I was a vision in black and we'd laughed together as I followed up with "And you took your medication when?" Yes—that was me. Always looking for a laugh. Why *didn't* I ask him how he felt when the doctor said his test results showed he was in the early stages of dementia? Why didn't I talk to him about what this would mean to him? The closest I came to being outright honest was the night he didn't know who I was and in order to get him into bed, I told him that I was his wife, and that he had a disease that prevented him from remembering. But those brief conversations, I think now, were not enough. I wish I hadn't buried my head in the sand and just carried on. I wish I had spent less time "handling" his needs and more time discovering them.

If I had it to do over again, I would have organized his to-do list less often and spent more time in meaningful conversation with him instead, especially the first couple of years after diagnosis, when his dementia hadn't progressed very far yet. I also deeply regret not being there the night he died. When I think about that or see something on television about a family with someone who's dying, I well up. I wish I had sat with him, holding his hand as his spirit finally moved on to peace. I hope my spirit will find peace around this.

Before I fall back to sleep, Don pops into my head. That happens fairly often when I'm up and awake too. Did I mention before that Don is a neat freak? Everything in its place? Mr. Private Person is also Mr. Tidy. You don't hang around with someone for three years without picking up some of their habits, and sometimes I laugh at myself as I straighten the forks in my cutlery drawer or routinely (now) put the coffee grinder back in the cupboard after use. *Don would approve of that.* But in the quiet of the night I ask myself, do I feel guilty that I let myself get involved with another man so soon after Bill died? My answer is no. I don't feel guilty. When people are in the various stages of grief and loss, they tend to grab on to anything that looks like a pain reliever—anything that will take them out of the situation they're in. For some, that relief can come from alcohol or drugs. For me it was Don. Note: This is just my thought. I have not checked out this idea with any professionals.

But yet another question looms. Was getting involved with Don—or with anyone, for that matter—so quickly after Bill died the wrong thing to do? Yes, I think it was. Being with Don took me out of my situation too soon. It delayed my ability to work through my feelings and move forward. Now, after five years, I've finally adjusted to living on my own and have learned to enjoy my own company. The funny thing is, I realize I had never lived alone until Bill died. I went from living with my parents to living with roommates to husband number one, to living just with Dianne, and then with Bill.

My sleepless journey then turns to the many roles of motherhood I have experienced in my life. Over time, I went from being a young, confident, and independent caregiver of a child to the head cheerleader and proud supporter of an accomplished married daughter and mother herself. Then I became an emotionally troubled parent who couldn't figure out why it looked like her daughter suddenly didn't seem to care about her. However, time can be a good healer. As can late-night musings. An interesting thing I have finally concluded about adult children—or at least about *my* adult offspring—is that they are not younger clones of us. They don't think like we do. They think and react for themselves based on their own life experiences and their individual situations. They may look like us and have family traits that reveal to anyone we meet that we're related. But they are not junior replicas. Being a daughter myself, you'd think I would have known that.

After Bill died, I mistakenly expected Dianne to think just like me. To react like me and to understand what I was feeling. But how could she? She had never lost a spouse or found herself suddenly living alone. She had never had to turn to her own children for help and support. So how could she intuitively know how to handle the emotional needs of her grieving mother? Worse, why did I assume that she would? Looking back on that time, I wonder if she was grieving as well. I bet she was. She really loved Bill. We never talked about that. Maybe it's time for more beer and wings. Or maybe not. Time to move on? Our problems were not anyone's fault. They just were what they were.

The storm outside having abated, I stretch out under the covers, nudging Charlie from one side of the bed to the other, and smile to myself. The decade since Bill and I moved from the condo to the country was not a journey I had planned for or one I would have chosen under "normal" circumstances. But having lived through it, it was a trip I wouldn't have missed. Living in rural Abbotsford gave me the opportunity to love and care for Bill while discovering the wonders of collecting farm-fresh eggs, learning the behavioural psychology of horses, and confirming that I was not cut out to be a market gardener. I will never again drive past a barn on a rural road or see horses in a field wearing their winter blankets without smiling. Today, spending serious money to buy a hothouse tomato at the grocery store makes me pine for the delicious crop of beefsteaks I was able to successfully grow on the back deck. In addition, the opportunity to get to know my grown-up daughter better, adult to adult, would not have happened with seventy-odd kilometres of highway between us. And living close by gives me the chance to keep hugging "my boys" every chance I get. That's a real gift.

Getting back into a strata situation was the right move. When I crossed the new threshold, with moving boxes in hand, I stopped being anxious about the next ten years, or the ten after that. I'm still not. I am curious about what is coming next and look forward to finding opportunities where I can make a difference or be useful, opportunities that will arise because I'm watching for them. I hate to sound so trite, but I like the expression "Bloom where you're planted." I think it's a fitting mantra for someone who's still not good at gardening.

RESOURCES

Alzheimer Society of B.C.
604-681-6530
alzheimerbc.org
info@alzheimerbc.org

* * *

Alzheimer Society of Canada
416-488-8772
alzheimer.ca
info@alzheimer.ca

* * *

British Columbia Bereavement Helpline
604-738-9950; toll free 1-877-779-2223
bcbh.ca
contact@bcbh.ca

* * *

Family Caregivers of British Columbia
250-384-0408; toll-free 1-877-520-3267
familycaregiversbc.ca

ABOUT THE AUTHOR

PAULINE BUCK is a retired public relations consultant who worked with a variety of not-for-profit, corporate, and entertainment clients in Vancouver, BC, in her thirty–year career. She was a senior account executive with one of Vancouver's most respected PR firms and later proprietor of her own public relations business. In addition, she served on volunteer boards including the Canadian Public Relations Society Vancouver, the Lions Gate Medical Research Foundation, and Vancouver AM Tourist Services Association, as president during the organization's early years. Her writing has appeared in various media, including CBC Radio, the *Globe and Mail,* and the *Vancouver Sun.*

A divorced single parent for most of the 1970s, Pauline raised her daughter on her own in North Vancouver until she met and married Bill Buck, who became much-loved husband number two and the best "dad" ever. Pauline continues to support community initiatives as a member and past president of the Rotary Club of Aldergrove and is involved on the social committee within the townhouse complex where she lives. She also plays bridge (badly) with three friends who gather weekly to drink coffee, catch up on the latest news, and occasionally play a hand or two. A proud grandmother, Pauline lives in Abbotsford with her golden doodle Charlie, a companion that keeps her "up and at 'em" in all weather.

Manufactured by Amazon.ca
Bolton, ON